Disclaimer

The accuracy of the information within this book is subject to change.

There is mentions of brands and facts stated within the book, may change as this book ages.

The content of this book may become inaccurate as time goes on. It is advised that you check when the book was purchased against the year of the book release date.

Okay now you can enjoy!

Gain infinite wisdom and be the best vegan this land has ever seen.

Figure 1 http://www.clipartpanda.com/categories/cow-clip-art-black-and-white (Accessed: June 17)

Special Thanks

A special thank you to the wonderful Kayleigh Blyth for designing the beautiful cover for this book, this is the second cover you have made for me and every time I am so happy with the result!

A big thank you to my dear friend Zoe Clydesdale for editing this book and putting up with all my typos, out of order lists and half started sentences.

Finally, a thank you to everyone who has followed my journey in making this book and has supported me in the process!

Especially the group of individuals in We love (and stan) Javier in this house!

Contents

- Seasonal Fruit & Veg
- Making New Meals
- Nutrients in Fruit & Veg

Beauty & Hygiene
- Top Tips
- Make Up
- False Eyelashes
- Bath & Shower Products
- Deodorants
- Skin Care
- Dental Care
- Perfumes
- Vitamin Tablets
- Extra Vegan bathroom Treats
- The Vegan Life Hack

House & Home
- Cleaning Products
- Laundry Products
- Cleaning Tools
- Other Vegan Household Products
- DIY Vegan Cleaners
- Vegan Candles

Human/Other Ethics
- Ethical Clothing Companies
- Fairtrade
- Palm Oil
- Plastic Usage Reduction

Questions about Veganism Answered

- Some Vegan Life Advice
- Questions you might Ponder as a Vegan
- Debunking the most common Anti-Vegan arguments
- How Veganism makes a Difference

La Fin

Means of Contacting

- Twitter - @amyythevegan
- Instagram - @amykennedywriting
- Email – amykennedypoetry@hotmail.com

Introduction

Hi! I'm Amy Kennedy, also known as @Amyythevegan on twitter (which is probably where you are coming from, if so hello welcome). As of this very moment I am 20 years old and have been vegan for just over two years, before this I was vegetarian for about four years. I'm pretty good at living a well-rounded balanced vegan life. I have faced a lot of health issues during my life which I have naturally cured, such as; polycystic ovary syndrome (PCOS), chronic migraines, acid reflux, Irritable bowel syndrome (IBS) and hair thinning all with the help of veganism.

I have spent the past two and a half years researching the vegan diet and actually living through what the lifestyle can achieve for you, so you could argue that I know my shit. To be honest, you could also argue I don't compared to someone who has the experience of being a vegan for twenty plus years but unfortunately, I have not lived long enough to compete with that. So I will give you my personal advice and life experience in a hope it can help other vegans or anyone transitioning or interested. At this point you are probably wondering what you are reading and why you're hearing about my life so I'll just get into the book now shall I?

Welcome to this book, I hope you find it helpful, feel free to speak to me about it and anything you find you still want some help with, I'll try my best to be a friendly face, and if I cannot help, I'll send you in the direction of somebody who can.

So, I was going to start this book all formal, but I voted against it as, to put it frank, I am not a professional, I am *not* a nutritionist, and I am not fully qualified with a degree in veganism (which probably isn't thing but just play along so you can see my point, ok?). I wanted to create a simple guide for you, the new vegan, the vegan, the person who is interested in cutting out meat, or the person who just knows a vegan and thought 'oh that's a nice little book I'm sure they'll read that and 100% not leave that on their shelf for years'. This is a guide to veganism, for the average person, so don't be expecting smoothie bowls so beautiful that it makes you reconsider your whole life in this book. You should be anticipating a nice guide to be a normal human who just wants to do their bit for their health, the animals, the planet, or whatever your reasoning may be, I'm here for it and it is valid.

Let's ease you into this book with a bit of light-heartedness, there are lots of types of vegans, because as with everything and everyone, we need to define ourselves as deeply as we possibly can. So here is a list of the types of vegan, just so you can pop it in your Instagram bio.

Plant Based

Doesn't eat animal products and that's the extent of their love for animals.

Junk Food Vegan

Lives of 'technically vegan' foods. Loves Oreos, bread, dips and crisps. 100% is drinking fizzy drinks over water.

The Gym Lad Vegan

Body is a temple not a graveyard. Does everything for the gains. Fitter than you will ever be.

Rawtil4

Only eats raw foods until 4pm... self-explanatory... probably loves yoga.

Completely Raw Vegan

Does not like hot food. Probably burned their mouth on a hot tomato when they were younger. Life motto is 'never trust a hot tomato'.

Soy Boy

Male vegan who just knows he doesn't feel the need for 'cow tittie milk'.

Instagram Vegan

Every meal is beautiful. Has more life aspirations than the average human.

The Casual Vegan

Just doesn't want animals to suffer. Doesn't care about following a diet. Very chill person. Stops to fuss every single dog they can.

The Argumentative Vegan

Gets a kick from arguing with meat eaters. Is always right. Brilliant for new information.

The Militant Vegan

Up everyone's ass about everything. Somehow everything you do makes you non-vegan. 10/10 vegan stereotype. 0/10 do not desire to be this.

There are definitely more than the above mentioned, but I want to guide you that there is more than one type of vegan. The whole purpose of that nice little list was not only just to tell you who you shouldn't be (the militant vegan) but to show you that veganism is not limited to just eating lettuce. You may be coming into this book thinking you will turn into one of these militant vegans, I promise you (unless that is your goal) you won't. Veganism is a personal journey and you can respond to it, talk about it and act on it in whatever ways you wish. Veganism is so much broader than everyone thinks, you do still have food options. Veganism is just making the decision to not eat anything that is from another animal. You can still be high in protein or healthy, you can still eat as much crap as you want, or you can carry on just not caring what you eat. You are not limited to just sitting around eating the same meals day in day out.

The Beginning

Part One - Why go Vegan?

Now you are fully aware of the ways you *could* categorise yourself, it is time for you to learn a little bit more. If you have got to the point where you are buying books about veganism, you probably have some idea about why you would like to go vegan or why you are already vegan. However, if you are in the small percentage who hasn't, or if you would just like a bit of wider knowledge to back up your personal reasonings, I will talk you through some of the best/most popular reasons. This normally breaks down to three things; your health, the animals and the environment. All these reasons are just as valid as each other and you can be vegan in your own way! I'm going to take this section to highlight some of the facts and figures behind each of these reasons. Now, this section may feel a bit heavy, but I promise the book will lighten up after this! This is an important part of the book as we need know our reasoning behind what we are doing. Unfortunately, the vegan lifestyle is still under some attack (I'll address coping with that later); but when you can come forward with the understanding, the facts and the figures, it makes it slightly easier for you to stand your ground!

Let's talk about Health;

I would like to start this little section of facts of by saying vegan does not equal healthy. You can follow a very junk food dense diet as a vegan. These facts on vegan lifestyle only apply if you are actively trying to live a healthy lifestyle with a well-balanced diet and exercise.

Nutrients and the vegan diet

Contrary to popular belief (i.e random people on twitter who suddenly have a degree in nutrition when you say you are vegan) the diet is in fact very nutrient dense. One study found that 'Vegans had the highest intakes of fibre, vitamin B1, folate, vitamin C, vitamin E, magnesium and iron'[1] in comparison to meat-eaters, pescatarians and vegetarians.

Weight Loss and Weight Management

A lot of people have reported that going vegan has helped them naturally lose weight. This is without putting the same levels of effort they would've needed to prior veganism. For example, I personally (to date) have lost 25lbs since going vegan. Without having any changes to my exercise routines. One study on postmenopausal women found that, even without portion controls, the plant-based diet was an affective way to lose weight.[2] In 2015 a study compared an omnivore diet to a vegan diet over a six-month period found that the vegan diet had a greater amount of weight loss and those who consumed less animal products were more likely to lose greater amounts of weight over the six-month period[3]

Lowering Blood Sugar and Aiding with Diabetes Management

There have been several studies into type-2 diabetes and the vegan diet that have emphasised how veganism can aid in management of the condition. A study conducted over four years

[1] Key et al, *Lifestyle characteristics and nutrient intakes in a cohort of 33 883 meat-eaters and 31 546 non-meat-eaters in the UK. Public Health Nutrition*, 6(3), (London: EPIC–Oxford, 2003) P259-268. (accessed 03/06/18)

[2] Barnard et Al, *The effects of a low-fat, plant-based dietary intervention on body weight, metabolism, and insulin sensitivity,* (Washington University:USA,2005) P991-997 (Accessed 04/06/18)

[3] Moore et Al, *Dietary adherence and acceptability of five different diets, including vegan and vegetarian diets, for weight loss: The New DIETs study,* (University of Carolina:USA, 2015), (Accessed 04/06/18)

found that the vegetarian and vegan diet were excellent and helping to control type-2 diabetes.[4]

Prevention/Protection from Cancer

The vegan diet has had a great link to preventing cancer and some individuals have even reported that is has helped them reverse or 'cure' their cancer[5]. This link has been supported by several studies and research is still ongoing to support these reports. One meta-analysis of several studies found that by going vegetarian or vegan you lower your risks of getting cancer[6]. Another US based study compared the affects of the vegetarian and vegan diet to that of a meat eater and found very similar results[7].

Symptom relief for Osteoarthritis

Studies have been conducted into the affect that a plant-based diet may have on the symptoms of arthritis and how it may be of aid. This was due to many people who go vegan reporting a change in their symptoms as the lifestyle change can be supported with these studies. One study found that those following a plant-

---

[4] Tonstad, Serena et al, *Type of Vegetarian Diet, Body Weight, and Prevalence of Type 2 Diabetes*, (Diabetes Care 32.5, 2009) P791–796. (Accessed 04/06/18)

[5] Nagelberg, Bobby, *Plant-Based Diet Helps 21 Year Old Recover From Brain Cancer*, 01/02/2017, https://nutritionstudies.org/plant-based-diet-helps-21-year-old-recover-from-brain-cancer/ (Accessed 03/06/2018)

[6] Abbate et al, *Vegetarian, vegan diets and multiple health outcomes: A systematic review with meta-analysis of observational studies*, 06/02/16, https://www.tandfonline.com/doi/full/10.1080/10408398.2016.1138447 (Accessed 03/06/18)

[7] Tantamango-Bartley, Yessenia et al. *VEGETARIAN DIETS AND THE INCIDENCE OF CANCER IN A LOW-RISK POPULATION.* (Cancer epidemiology, biomarkers & prevention: a publication of the American Association for Cancer Research, cosponsored by the American Society of Preventive Oncology 22.2, 2013) P286–294. https://www.ncbi.nlm.nih.gov/pmc/articles/PMC3565018/ (Accessed 03/06/18)

based diet had a more significant relief from symptoms than a control group.[8]

Later in the book you will see I have gathered a lot more on individual's journeys into to veganism! These stories are by real people just like me and you, not people in a study. I find it helpful to listen to how other people have found veganism as an aid to their health, as it adds a sense of reality. Veganism is still *extremely* understudied. There are people with conditions that they can tell have improved but cannot find any evidence to back themselves up!

Don't worry if I've discussed conditions you don't have, or conditions you haven't heard off! These are just areas that have had some form of research into! This is also no way a disclaimer that veganism will 100% be your cure! Some people find no change in health, others report gradual change, and others say they experience immediate change! Everyone has personal experiences with veganism!

Veganism and the animals

A very popular reason to go vegan is to end senseless animal suffering. Pigs, cows, chicken and sheep are extraordinarily smart and social animals and the conditions that they live in often cause the animals a lot of emotional trauma and stress. The best way to understand how you *should* feel when seeing the animals in this condition; is looking at how you react when you see dogs, cats and other domestic animals who are in small cages, malnourished, evidently sad, scared and isolated. If seeing a domestic animal this way upsets and enrages you, then seeing farm animals should

---

[8] Clinton et Al, *Whole-Foods, Plant-Based Diet Alleviates the Symptoms of Osteoarthritis,* (Michigan:USA, 2015), (Accessed 04/06/18)

provoke the same reaction in you. Once you have connected that food on your plate to an animal that deserves to live it becomes very hard to disassociate the two. Below is going to be some facts and figures about the affect agriculture has on animals, some may find this upsetting so feel free to skip this section if you want to!

Over 56 billion animals are killed per year by humans (not including fish & sea creatures).[9]

Male chicks are deemed as useless within the egg industry, so they are killed by means such as; suffocation, gassing or mincing at the mere age of a day old.[10]

Dairy cows are forcibly inseminated for the females to produce milk, and their babies are taken away from them with almost immediate notice. Cows also have a much shorter life span as it has been reported 'cows can live for up to 25 years, the vast majority of 'dairy' cows are killed at around 5 years old, when their milk production drops and they are considered 'spent' by the industry.'[11]

Beef cows are often killed between the ages of two and three.[12]

Pigs are often slaughtered between the ages of 1.5 months and 4 months depending on the meat[13]

Chickens are often placed into sheds with little to no room to move. They are bred very quickly, in a means that also makes them very unhealthy, this makes them 'ready for slaughter so

---

[9] https://www.animalequality.net/food (Accessed 04/06/18)

[10] Ibid

[11] Ibid

[12] http://www.fao.org/docrep/004/T0279E/T0279E05.htm (Accessed 04/06/18)

[13] Ibid & https://en.wikipedia.org/wiki/Pig_slaughter (Accessed 04/06/18)

quickly that their legs often cannot support the weight of their bodies, and many suffer heart attacks'.[14]

Most cows experience several illnesses due to the conditions they live in, this includes; Mastitis, Lameness, ketosis, hypocalcaemia, BSE Bovine Spongiform Encephalopathy (BSE), Bovine Tuberculosis (bTB), Foot and Mouth and pneumonia[15]

The Environment

Animal agriculture is having a great effect on our environment. This is not something that is sustainable with our growing population. Below is a list of facts, in a very similar way to the two lists you've already seen (no need to act shocked I know it is revolutionary).

The dairy industry uses excessive amounts of water in comparison to plant-based milks. It has been reported that on average it 'takes 30 gallons of water to make one glass of milk, 50 gallons of water to make two slices of cheese, and a whopping 109 gallons of water to make one stick of butter.'[16] Whereas one glass of soy takes 9 gallons of water and one glass of almond milk takes 23 gallons. [17]

It takes 2,400 gallons of water to produce a mere one pound of meat, whereas, it takes 25 gallons to produce a pound of wheat. Which means not eating one pound of meat would be the equivalent of saving the water from six months of showers (so please, cut the meat out and keep on showering). It has also been found that half on the water in the US is put towards the meat industry. [18]

---

[14] https://www.animalequality.net/food (Accessed 04/06/18)
[15] https://www.vegsoc.org/page.aspx?pid=561 (Accessed 04/06/18)
[16] https://mercyforanimals.org/12-facts-you-probably-didnt-know-about-dairy (Accessed 04/06/18)
[17] https://www.motherjones.com/environment/2014/03/california-water-suck/ (Accessed 04/06/18)
[18] https://www.peta.org/features/meat-climate-change/ (Accessed

It has been found that animal agriculture releases more green house gas emissions than all the exhausts from transportation. Animal agriculture is responsible for 18% of greenhouse gases.[19] The effects of animal agriculture can be reversed as it has recently been discussed that 'if the US reduced meat consumption by 50%, it's the equivalent of taking 26 million cars off the road.'[20] Let's not lie to ourselves, cutting down your meat intake by 50% is not too much to ask.

Animal agriculture has been found to be responsible for a whopping 51% of all worldwide greenhouse gases as livestock and their by-product are responsible for a minimum of 32,000 million tons of carbon dioxide.[21]

I'm sure we've all heard the fact that 'an area the size of a football pitch is cut down every minute in the rainforest' and nobody ever thought to ask why? Well, so it would seem, animal agriculture is responsible for a great deal of it. With reports that 'an estimated 70 percent of deforestation in the Amazon basin can be attributed to cattle ranching.'[22] Not only is the land being used to actual *home* the cattle, being used to grow the crops to feed them. As we learnt earlier, we could use these crops for food, with half the environmental consequences.

04/06/18)

[19] http://www.fao.org/docrep/010/a0701e/a0701e00.HTM (Accessed 04/06/18)

[20] Cameron, James, *Animal agriculture is choking the Earth and making us sick. We must act now,* Dec 2017, https://www.theguardian.com/commentisfree/2017/dec/04/animal-agriculture-choking-earth-making-sick-climate-food-environmental-impact-james-cameron-suzy-amis-cameron (Accessed 04/06/18)

[21] http://www.cowspiracy.com/facts/ (Accessed 04/06/18)

[22] Sarma, Priyakshi, *Beef Production is Killing the Amazon Rainforest,* March 2014. https://www.onegreenplanet.org/animalsandnature/beef-production-is-killing-the-amazon-rainforest/ (Accessed 04/06/18)

A lot of people forget about the fact that fishing has on the planet. It's important here to note that we have a very delicate eco system. There are very specific food change within the laws of the sea, and us overfishing can very easily affect other marine life. I'm sure we have all seen the video of whales, dolphins and other sea life literally chasing fishing boats.

It has been argued that almost half the fish we catch gets discarded as it is deemed as no good for human consumption (i.e. it is just random sea life that we did not intend on catching, we just happened to have it in our nets). This makes the scene in finding nemo where Dory gets caught in the net all too real. It has been recently reported that in some cases less that half of the fish we catch is used by humans, the rest is simply wasted.[23]

If you have thoroughly enjoyed learning about the environment there are loads more facts about how animal agriculture affects the planet on this website - http://www.cowspiracy.com/facts/. You'll find the more you investigate the affects of animal agriculture on the planet the greater the responsibility you feel when making choices in eating. When one burger equates to six months of showering, and one fish equates to several others dying without purpose, it becomes a lot easier to place the responsibility into your own hands.

There you have it, some (arguably) harsh truths about animal agriculture and how we can save our health, the planet and the animals by going vegan! Now you've been shown a mere snippet of what veganism can help, I hope you are feeling a bit more fuel for your fire! Facts and knowledge are very important when it comes to veganism, to help you in this lifestyle change you like to have your beliefs reinforced with some good hard facts. As I just mentioned, this is just scratching the surface. I could bore you

---

[23] http://www.fao.org/docrep/W6602E/w6602E09.htm (Accessed 04/06/18) - attached is a collections of studies that explore the waste within fishing.

with endless facts and figures, but I won't be doing that today unfortunately. Now, I can send you on your way and you can do some independent research and see what you might discover! I know this part of going vegan can be very intimidating, but just remember to take your time and move at a pace that is comfortable for you. The most important thing about veganism is the fact that you are willing to try. Some people go vegan overnight, others take months or even years until they reach their full vegan form! As long as you are putting in your best efforts, there is nothing else that you can expect from yourself other than that!

Part Two - What to Watch?

Now you have some basic knowledge we are moving on to arguably the most important part of your vegan journey. The getting some wider information and background knowledge part. This is the bit where you have a proper rummage around veganism and see where it takes you. There are lots of ways to go about this, personally I find documentaries are the best way to find an understanding of veganism. There are absolutely loads of informative documentaries and videos out there, and you will find the more you watch the more you know. With the more you know, the more likely you are to commit to the lifestyle. Like anything you do in life, you normally have a reason. Veganism is the same (shock horror) so when you find your reason to committing to the lifestyle, you will find it a lot easier than you did before. I've prepared a nice little list for you of documentaries you might find helpful. As of this date most of these are accessible on YouTube or Netflix so have a little google!

Some of these have got graphic scenes so make sure you investigate this if it will upset you or distress you.

Blackfish (2013) - Gabriela Cowperthwaite

Carnage (2017) - Simon Amstell

Cowspiracy (2014) – Kip Andersen

Crazy Sexy Cancer (2007) - Kris Carr

Dominion (2018) - Chris Delforce & Joaquin Phoenix

Earthlings (2005) – Shaun Monson & Joaquin Phoenix

Forks Over Knifes (2011) – Lee Fulkerson

Food Choices (2016) - Michal Siewierski

Land of Hope and Glory (2017) – Eathling Ed

Live and Let Live (2013) - Marc Pierschel

What The Health (2017) – Kip Andersen

Vegan Everyday Stories (2016)

Vegucated (2011) - Marisa Miller Wolfson

This is my list of the top 12 documentaries to watch. There are many more out there, but this is the twelve that I believe are most commonly discussed, known or talked about. Feel free to have a little browse through and see what takes your fancy; but please just remember some do have graphic scenes that can be very upsetting to watch. Do not put yourself in a situation where you will become distressed. There are plenty of documentaries out there that you can gain a lot from without being made uncomfortable or uneasy.

Part Three - Helpful Websites

The internet is a very broad and terrifying place if you aren't too sure what you are looking for. Well I'm here to offer you, once again, a little bit of guidance. There are lots of vegan websites out there! With recipes, cruelty free make up, cruelty free cleaning products, accidental vegan foods, good ethical clothing companies, how to make your own vegan cheese and many, many more. The list is never ending. If you are struggling or confused about something, there will be someone out there who also struggled with it, enough to make a nice little guide for you. One of the things that helped me with my journey into veganism was bookmarking a heck of a lot of websites. Websites about literally everything. Whether it is recipes or just vegan news, I have it pinned. This list below is a list of some websites I found particularly handy. I should remind you, that these are websites that I personally enjoy. Everyone else finds different things useful, and this is just something I see as a very good way to explore veganism, what it means, and what it is achieving! So once again, feel free to have a browse.

https://www.bosh.tv/

https://www.livekindly.co/

https://www.plantbasednews.org/

http://fatgayvegan.com/

https://www.vegansociety.com/

http://vegnews.com/

https://veganwomble.co.uk/

https://minimalistbaker.com/

https://goveganworld.com/

http://www.onegreenplanet.org/

These websites cover a variety of things whether it be easy meals, new studies, new foods or new products! There are changes to the vegan lifestyle everyday and it is becoming more and more accessible! Hopefully you'll have a look at these websites and see what the lifestyle has to offer you. You will not have to give up your favourite meals, your hobbies or your favourite restaurants (unless it is a steakhouse in which case you might struggle). In case you haven't guessed it yet, I am starting this book with a lot of lists. Lists are just a handy way for you to quickly get the information you need, because lets not lie to ourselves; nobody wants to sit and read a 100 page book about veganism when I could just give it to you in a load of unintimidating lists that you can highlight or scribble on. I'm not one to beat around the bush or try and drag out things, you've brought this book because you want to go vegan, or you want to make steps towards veganism, and I am not about to give you a novel and make the journey harder.

Part Four - Vegan YouTubers

A big way for people to gain casual knowledge these days is through YouTube! The videos are normally small and safe so nobody is overwhelmed by a sudden influx of knowledge. Here are some YouTubers who post things about veganism or are dedicated vegan channels!

Apples and Amanda

Cheap Lazy Vegan

Earthling Ed

ETHCS

Hench Herbivore

Highcarb Hannah

JAKD VEGANS

Jenna and Julien (They cook a lot of vegan foods)

Josef Lincoln

Liv B

Maddie Lymburner

Naturally Stefanie

PLANT BASED NEWS

Plantriotic

Sweet Potato Soul

Supreme Banana

Stella Rae

Sonia Elsie

Tess Begg

That Vegan Couple

Part Five - The Best Vegan Apps

Vegan apps can help make your life 100% easier! So here are some, I would recommend for making your transition (and life) easier.

BunnyFree – This app shows you beauty/cosmetics that are cruelty free.

CodeCheck – This app helps you find vegan foods, cosmetics and household products with personalised settings.

Happy Cow – This app shows you restaurants with vegan options.

Is it Vegan? – This does what it says on the tin... It'll tell you if a product is vegan.

Veggiebeers – Making sure your booze is safe.

Part Six - Vegan Books I Recommend

A lot of people find that stacking their shelves with information is their preferred way of knowledge (that might be why you brought a physical version of this book!) So below I'm going to list some of the most renowned books about veganism! I haven't read all of these books myself personally (although I am getting around to it), take a look at them and once again if any of them take your fancy see if you can get your hands on them.

How Not To Die - Michael Greger MD

Greger (a nutrition expert) shows us the foods that will help us fight and reverse diseases.

The China Study – T. Collin Campbell

A look into one of the most comprehensive studies ever conducted into nutrition.

The Forks Over Knifes Plan - Alona Pulde and Matthew Lederman

A four-week plan to help you transition into a plant-based diet.

Becoming Vegan – Brenda Davis

A look into the nutrients and diet plans of a plant-based diet.

Eating Animals - Jonathan Safran Foer

A discussion into whether or not we *should* be eating animals.

Cheese Trap - Neal Barnard MD

A look into why and how 'cheese addiction' becomes a reality and what it does to our health.

Minimalist Baker Everyday Cooking - Dana Shultz

An easy to follow vegan cookbook.

Why We Love Dogs, Eat Pigs and Wear Cows – Melanie Joy

A discussion into speciesism and why we treat animals in different ways.

This is just a small percentage of the vegan books that are out there. You can find books about health, animals the environment, being a fitness fanatic and vegan. Books on how to cook vegan and even vegan story books for kids. Find what *you* think will inspire you the most and hit the ground running.

Vegan Stories from Real Vegans

Part One - Introduction

This section of the book is dedicated to other people's stories. I reached out on my twitter to my followers to ask them to tell me their stories, about what veganism has done for them, why they went vegan and how they went vegan. I can show you studies for hours and hours but hearing from real life people like you and me makes veganism that much more real.

You are about to read a lot of different people's experiences and I can almost guarantee you that all these people are from different walks of life. I hope that through reading all these stories you will be able to see that you do not need to be a certain type of person in order to go vegan. You don't have to be an activist, you don't have to have money, you even don't have to be an animal lover to go vegan!

So, please, get yourself a nice cup of tea, a nice little snack and get comfortable. These reads are going to be very diverse and hopefully very helpful for you! Those who are brave enough to show their identity will more than likely have their twitter handle next to their story! I'm sure they will be willing to help you with anything (if you are to relate to their story particularly) so if you have the courage to message, make sure to do so. Enjoy!

Part Two - Personal Story

Hi, we touched on my story in the beginning and now I would like to sit and talk about myself for a while if that is quite alright? If it isn't I suggest you just skip this part because I'm going to do it anyway.

I have been vegan for two years now, and it has changed my life in more ways then I could've ever imagined it could (that's right get out your tissues this one is going to be deep). My parents have always said to me that they struggled to get me to eat anything to do with animals, so I think it was something I was destining to do. I had a dog for the first eight years of my life who was my best friend, and when I lost him I knew that animals were equal to humans, I was just too young and too uneducated to connect the dots between the pet I considered a friend and a chicken I had never met nor seen. It wasn't until almost ten years later that I connect the idea of friendship and compassion to animals we see as 'food'.

When I transitioned to vegetarianism I thought I was doing more than enough for the animals. At that point in my life, I had no idea of the cruelty that went into the eggs and dairy industries, it wasn't until I actually started looking into veganism for my health that I learnt that the animals were suffering in ways that was too cruel for me to ignore.

I initially went vegan for my health. I had been suffering with chronic migraines, IBS, Acid Reflux and polycystic ovaries for quite some time and the doctors never managed to find a cure, only things that would temporarily relieve symptoms. I made the decision that I was going to investigate this veganism malarkey and I did it the only way I knew how, Netflix and YouTube. I gradually started learning more and more about the affects animal products had on the planet, the animals and my body and I decided that enough was enough and I was going to start my journey.

I transitioned over the space of about a month or two with my food and to this day I am still working out and working in products within my home and life, now you see why I'm all for the steady transition right? I found myself finding it easier and easier every day and my migraine symptoms relieved within weeks. I used to have a migraine at least once a month and since going vegan I have had three in two years. With my IBS and Acid Reflux I found that within a month I was off my tablets completely! I found that my body had regulated how it reacts to foods and drinks and that I was able to manage it for myself!

So, this is the big one for me here, PCOS. I found within three to four months that my PCOS almost entirely reversed and I managed to get my weight to become stable, my hair began to grow more healthy and thick and my period pains even relieved over time. PCOS is something I have been diagnosed with for over twelve years at this point (2018) and I have never been offered a lot of help! Unfortunately, PCOS is something that doctors don't necessarily know the cure or cause too so you can only imagine the joys that I felt as I saw the symptoms slowly disappear. In a similar fashion to my migraines I do still get the occasional hormone flare up, and by occasional, I mean genuinely once or twice a year. It feels incredible to not have PCOS being such a predominate part of my life anymore, and I do owe it all to veganism. Veganism has even helped me to steadily lose weight, something my body has more often than not refused to humour. Physically veganism has changed a lot about who I am and how I see myself, and it has never made me happier! Mentally veganism has given me this new drive and a new passion. I feel inspired to spread the message about something I care about very deeply. Personally, veganism is the best thing I have ever done, it has changed everything in my life for the better and every day I am learning and growing because of it.

For me personally, I see veganism as a way of extending your compassion and allowing yourself to truly be at one with this earth that we are lucky enough to live on. You are reminded that you are an equal, and that you will come and go on this earth alongside the animals you meet on the journey, you are reminded that your time is limited, so you might as well be as gentle and as kind as you can be.

Part Three - Stories from Fellow Vegans

Here we have a collection of stories from fellow vegans! These are brought to you from a variety of different people with differences in their backgrounds, education and experience, so please bare that in mind as you read. I am quoting exactly (minus typos, thanks to my amazing editor) so please give them a read as you may find some stories that you relate too. Everyone's journey into veganism is different, and these stories should highlight to you that you do not have to do veganism a set way! We all go into it differently, see different results and experience different things.

'I stopped eating meat one day at school because I was in cooking class making pizza and my friend was putting sausage and bacon on hers and said "it's like I'm eating a whole pig". After that I went home, told my mum I was vegetarian and she said "well you've got spaghetti bolognaise for dinner". After that I never ate meat again and my mum was very supportive. Almost 10 years later and we're both vegan now 😊' - **@TashaCaitlinn**

'I was watching Okja whilst eating a kebab, that's my story ☐' - **@JAMIENAGEV**

'I started watching a YouTuber Morgan Joyce who is vegan and I got super interested I was 15 and going through tough times in my life and going vegan seemed like something I could take charge of. So I started cutting out one thing out each week like I would give up beef the first week then chicken. I never liked eggs so that was easy to give up so in about a month I had gone vegetarian I stayed vegetarian for about 6 months and I started education myself more on veganism I watched documentaries and videos of the cruel meat industry I had a reason to go vegan I didn't want anyone dying for my own taste.

So I went vegan, it was a very hard transition at first no one in my family knew what vegan was and I lived in a small city where there were no vegan restaurants. So basically for a year my food intake was potatoes, Oreos, chips and vegan hotdogs and pasta I did not try to learn to cook or anything I was very unhealthy I would fall asleep all the time just drink coffee and eat maybe 2 times a day just a bag of chips and soda.

Eventually I just gave up I didn't want to keep trying I put my own selfish feeling first my mentality was "who cares veganism never works I can eat what I want who is to tell me what I can and can't eat". I broke my veganism for a year and a half and then my sister who is younger than me went vegan and I started to watch she would cook nice meals and she just looked so happy and healthy so I decided to try it out again the same way I had the first time and I really started researching what exactly I needed and I wanted to be part of this community part of me felt so ashamed for breaking my veganism for so long but the more reading and videos and podcast I listened to and watched I realized this is a community that will accept you for what you are and that we are all trying to reach the same goal. I have been vegan for about almost 2 years, 2 of my sisters are vegan one is in transition to veganism I love cooking and trying new vegan places and it's not a burden! I love this community every day I learn more and more my goal this year is to become a vegan activist to help people learn the truth and save the animals! Veganism has changed my life in so many ways and it only gets better from here❤️ I AM VEGAN FOR LIFE!❤️' - **@desireedyani**

'My story is not very interesting, but I was bored one day so I decided to watch What The Health and I went vegan as soon as I was done watching it. I haven't looked back since.' - **@_evelynepender**

'I had (and still have) depression and anxiety but veganism definitely gave me a purpose in life and helps me realize that I don't have to feel like a waste and that I have potential to be part of something bigger than just me' – **Anon**

'I was diagnosed with IBS around the age of 17, after having tests for everything else done and was given medication and I don't really remember any discussions about my diet, vitamins or anything. For the next two years, I suffered with IBS on a daily basis, restricting my social life and feeling so self-conscious because I just never knew when the next attack would come, when the pain would come back or when I'd need the medication. And there was a lot of medication. It was during this time I was still eating meat and dairy.

Move forwards two years and I'm at university, feeling stressed which can set off IBS but I've been reading into how your diet impacts your gut and what the common triggers are for IBS sufferers. I decided to go vegan initially to help my IBS and I literally had no idea how much my health would improve. Honestly, the positives never stopped coming and I've never felt better. I no longer needed a lot of the medication, I still need some because my intestines sometimes go into spasm and nothing can control that, but medicine and it really hurts. Eating healthier and more fibre has made my IBS so much easier to live with. I've gone from having daily attacks to about one every two months - there's no cure for IBS, it's horrible at times but I manage so much better now. IBS is an invisible illness with so many side effects, including being lethargic and tired all the time but nothing makes me feel better than vegan food. Being vegan has helped me learn about nutrition, what my body needs and what is good for me. I regret all those years I ate meat and dairy, because now my IBS is better, my stomach pain is basically gone, I feel sick less often, I no longer feel so awful after a big meal, I feel healthier, my skin is better, I'm not reliant on medication anymore, I'm able to say yes to social occasions because I don't have to worry about my health and I've made loads of new friends, yourself included, and I'd never give up veganism for anything, it's changed my life and saved me in so many ways.' - **@smellykellymoo**

'My name is Allyson Reinert. I grew up in a conservative family full of meat heads. From being constantly fed stuff my dad cooked on the smoker, eventually when I was 16 I remember thinking it was just absolutely disgusting and I couldn't eat it anymore. I cut out red meat, but still loved chicken and all other animal products. A few months later, I had an amazing teacher who really inspired me to pursue environmental science as a career. So naturally I started doing a bunch of research on the environment and saw how animal agriculture affects it and basically went vegetarian overnight. Stayed like that for about 6 months until going vegan after watching videos on the dairy and egg industry.

So basically, vegetarian for the environment, vegan for the animals!!

My life has improved SO much since the transition. I suffer from chronic migraines so debilitating I almost failed school for absences all 8 semesters of high school. Once going vegan, instead of migraines almost every single day, it's about once every 2 weeks. Which is incredible for me. Also the mental clarity and how lightweight and healthy you feel naturally on a vegan diet' - @alllyson827

'When I was 11 I remember walking down the street with my friend and we were eating a bag of beef jerky. I made a comment to her about how I felt guilty that animals had to die for me to eat them. She told me how since they were going to be killed anyways it would do nothing and be a waste NOT to eat them. I believed her, that's my biggest regret. The guilt built up for the next few years as I continued to eat animal products. When I was 13, it was too much for me to handle and I went vegetarian. Like most people, I got a lot of backlash for it but I stuck with it. A little over a year later, when I was 14, my family went on a trip to Europe to visit friends. These friends made us a lot of home cooked meals and I remember one of them told me, "thank god you're vegetarian and not vegan, it would be a lot harder to cook for you. Plus I don't think you could stick with it." That was the last little push I needed and when I got home I went vegan and never looked back.' @_ _zhdtse

'I live in a rural mountain town (population less than 3000) in the Appalachian mountains in the USA. I had witnessed so much wildlife growing up but my story began with my grandmother when I was a child, maybe six or seven years old. Every moment with her was ethereal and so held more significance to my developing worldview, I guess you might say. My days were spent in her garden or playing in the creek behind her tiny secluded home in the forest while she painted landscapes and wrote poetry - life was picturesque and pain didn't exist in my mind. The day before Thanksgiving, she and I trekked the mountainside with a sled, clearing a path as we went from the rock and branches. When we reached the mountain top we were in witness of a pack of wild turkey and sat down to watch them for what seemed like an eternity. Though I'd seen wildlife before that moment, just being in their presence after that journey felt like a reward. They were so gorgeous and pure. As the sun began to set, we climbed into the sled and rode down the path we forged which marked the end to one of the most beautiful and exhilarating days of my life to that point. The next day, as customary for Thanksgiving, turkey was served for dinner. With my mind still swirling with the images of those beautiful creatures: a turkey lay dead, plucked, and beheaded on the table before me. I was devastated trying to reconcile these two images and the lingering high from the day before. The thought of eating animals had been a major ethical dilemma for me ever since. In my town and its culture, I was the first vegetarian I knew and started around thirteen years old after discovering slaughterhouse footage and animal activism sites. I distributed pamphlets in the school lunchroom and advocated petitions to stop the stores from selling fur, etc. Many of my friends stopped eating meat and started advocating with me. After years of back and forth, I finally took the step to becoming vegan with inspiration from a person I loved and looked up to at the age of twenty seven. I hate the fact it took so long after all the years of knowledge and ethical dilemma but now my conscious is finally clear. I'm healthier and happier than ever before, especially knowing no creature died or suffered for my fleeting pleasure. Moments like that day with my grandmother are not fleeting. It's easy to be disassociated when getting animal products is as easy as grabbing it off the shelf, pre-packaged, and without a face or a story. I'm not angry with those who do, I just wish our early exposure to animals was different than on a plate or in a package. It is desensitizing when animals are sold as commodities before us from as early as we can remember. It is never too late, though. I share vegan-cooked meals with reluctant others who otherwise wouldn't have ever considered a meal without animal products. They may not be vegan now but culture is changing and everything we, as vegans, do is an impact. I want to help people connect to the beauty of nature and its creatures rather than them connecting animals to a pleasure commodity. If you can, be that person who loves and shares ethereal moments with both people and animals and eventually things will fall into place.' - **Anon**

'So on the 2 June 2018 I was browsing YouTube and the thought of going vegan went through my head. I have thought about going vegan so many times before though but never took action also I was so young and everyone else in my family was well, carnivores. So I decided to post in my personal diary called twitter - where I can usually share whatever is on my mind and no one will judge me. I can't remember the exact words I tweeted but it went something like: So I've been thinking of going vegan recently but I don't know where to start and I don't know how my family will take this. A few minutes past and unknowingly my notifications filled with vegans all across the world messaging me and encouraging me to go vegan. I didn't feel alone anymore and I thought to myself 'OKAY JUST DO IT! ITS NOW OR NEVER' and ever since that day I haven't looked back. I started anxiously planning which foods I should get, grocery lists etc. This was made so much easier because the vegan community on twitter sent me various links and I went to them and it helped me complete a list of items I should get and also according to my budget. After all I am a 19 year old and the only one who's going to only eat plant based foods in the family. [...] Why I went vegan? I just love animals so much. I have two cats and a dog and I love them so much and I can't imagine any harm being done to them. No animal, even living on a farm should be treated the way animals are treated just for humans to be able to enjoy them as "food".' - **@imtiaz_isaacs**

'I grew up on a farm and always loved animals (or at least, I thought I did, I guess I didn't really since I was contributing to their slavery and slaughter). But my grandad always sold the animals on, he never actually brought them to the slaughterhouse directly, so I was kind of disconnected from that end of things. Like most people I never really thought of the consequences of my consumption. I always believed the myth that people needed meat to be healthy (oh my god, can I go back in time and punch myself? 😄). Like many vegans, what made me question it all was watching Cowspiricy and earthlings. I started to make the connection between what I was paying for and what it meant for animals. I done some research, figured out that a plant based diet was not only perfectly healthy but probably better for us, realised just how bad consuming animal products is for the environment and more importantly that I could stop contributing to this miserable system by becoming vegan 🌱 ' – **@veigeanach**

'I actually went vegan after watching documentaries like conspiracy, what the health, and because of my own experiences of seeing animals suffer and be treated horribly here in California's agriculture heart of the Central Valley. Once I took that step forward, there was no going back. I felt more fulfilled and happy then ever and my family noticed how I radiated. They thought it was because I had lost weight prior to transitioning but actually I just felt like a decent human being doing my part and that made me happy. Since then, my health has greatly improved. I have ADD and although I still require medication, I have noticed a great improvement in my ability to focus. I think the most interesting thing is that I had eczema since I was 14 years old (now 22), to the point of needing steroid creams and monthly self-injection shots full of steroids. But after becoming vegan, I have not had one single outbreak in a year.' - **@thealphazaida**

'So I would love to share my story even though it's not super crazy or anything because going vegan really changed my life.

It was my freshman year of high school and my physical science class was watching Food Inc. because we had a substitute. After watching that I was literally sick with what I was eating and where it came from. I went vegetarian that same day and I stayed that was for four years until one day I decided to go vegan for the Catholic Lenten season. I didn't haven't anyone to ask—or so I thought— so I struggled to find food but still didn't give up and just googled what I could and I've been vegan for a whole year now and is been the best thing that's ever happened to me. I've helped 3 people start their journey to veganism in the past year and it feels so good to know I'm making a difference no matter how small! Even though I am religious, I very much believe that my God put me on earth to do great things for these animals and even if someone isn't religious, doing it for the earth and for the animals is all that matters.' - **@ItsjuliaJulia**

'I was diagnosed with Rheumatoid Arthritis, Fibromyalgia, IBS and a few other gastrointestinal issues. I was on several medications for those illnesses as well as for pain and depression and inflammatory illnesses. I was lucky to be out of bed 2-3 days a month because I was so sick. I was missing out on life because I was in bed sick all the time. There were many times I was taken to the hospital by ambulance and many, many doctors to visit almost weekly. After reading about cutting dairy out of a diet helping someone I decided to try that. Soon I started to notice a very slight difference in the way I felt so I did some research and decided to add a few other things to my list of exclusions. I had been a vegetarian many years before so I thought I might try cutting out meat—except chicken and bacon because "I couldn't live without them". Over time I felt better and better and had less issues with Fibromyalgia and GI issues and my arthritis. After I started to make the connection that the majority of my problems were from my diet I went completely vegan. That was almost 3 years ago now and I'm happy to say that I'm on zero medications, I'm 100% free of any symptoms for ANY of my previous diagnoses and I'm no longer contributing to the decline of the planet or the massive cruelty I learned about during my vegan research. That one fact has resonated so hard with me out of any of the other benefits. I believe my soul has been cleansed of the negative emotions I absorbed from eating cruelly treated animals. I finally feel a sense of calm and wellness now. I can't stress how much it's changed my life both physically and mentally but it's been a literal life saver for me.' - **@stefrenchie**

'I was vegetarian first for 6/7 years and was totally unaware of how cruel the dairy and egg industry is. I remember thinking veganism seemed so extreme when one of my friends went raw vegan for a bit and honestly never thought I'd ever go vegan, especially as I was intolerant to gluten it was already restrictive being veggie. I slowly but surely cut out direct egg and dairy and still consumed some Quorn products that had those ingredients in. I started following more and more vegans on social media and YouTube and watched the documentaries they all recommended. After that I couldn't participate knowingly anymore. I went vegan in January 2018 as part of Veganuary and I haven't looked back since. My cooking has stepped up a notch and I am so more creative in the kitchen, I'm also not riddled with guilt anymore. I'm 100% vegan for the animals & environment the rest of the advantages are merely the cherry on top for me.' - **@hello_saralou**

'Basically I was around 10 when this happened, because I've been watching onision since I was 7-8. One day, I saw he put out a video about veganism, and I immediately watched it just outta curiosity. And it changed my life. I know this was very drastic, and reading this, I get that, but I was so determined to always do the most caring option for others.

And I did this by watching evidence to back up all sides, and just from seeing how cruel someone could be to innocent others, I really did not want to support that. It did, and still makes me sick to my stomach to this day.' - **@enamoredhowell**

'I actually became vegetarian before I was vegan and that was about a year ago today. The documentary "what the health" changed me, I quit eating meat, yogurt, eggs and cut wayyyy back on cheese and quit drinking cow's milk. I could feel such a shift in my body and soul but I still felt that heavy feeling when I ate cheese and ice cream. I had been wanting to go vegan quite soon after I went vegetarian and I was already pretty close to it. My boyfriend and I ate "almost vegan" for a while and I finally made the shift to full vegan on March 5th. I was born to live this life. I couldn't hurt animals any longer!' - **Anon**

'Hi! I started going vegan in July 2017 officially. I was always on and off vegetarian through high school, and after I took an AP environmental science class as well as watching What the Health I decided to make the switch. I stopped eating meat completely and phased dairy out over a span of a few months and in January of this year I went full vegan.' - **@Eggypencil**

'I met my girlfriend my sophomore year of college. I fell in love with how passionate she was about things, especially her compassion for all life and being a vegan. When we were just friends she got me thinking I could be a vegetarian, and I was for a while. Naturally though, some things get better with time and as our friendship grew into falling in love, my vegetarian became vegan. It was the best decision I've ever made right behind falling in love with her. 🥬🍴' - **@CourtneyNHudson**

'I've been vegetarian pretty much my whole life because I was raised that way and just want animals to be left in peace without humans killing them. When I was 19, a friend and I watched Cowspiracy and I was immediately hit by the environmental case for veganism and the inescapable cruelty of dairy.

Since becoming vegan, I've met so many passionate activists either at animal rights events, vegan festivals, or on social media, who constantly inspire me. Going vegan is honestly one of the best things I've ever done.' - **@acidzamo**

'I went vegan on my 16th birthday. Before being vegan I ate meat, then went pescetarian and then veggie. I always knew when I began my transition was that my aim was to end up vegan, and what really pushed me to becoming vegan was an article by The Guardian about the dairy industry and the environmental impacts it had. At dinner that night I said that's it, I'm going vegan. I have been ever since.

Before becoming vegan I used to hate cooking, but now, I love it! I can now really appreciate how creative you can be to make yummy vegan foods and prove to people that vegans don't live off lettuce🥬. Making yummy vegan foods that people enjoy, vegan junk food and puddings, is one way I'm trying to spread the vegan love. My main reason for being vegan is for the environment and animals. That is all i care about. The health benefits are just a bonus in my opinion. 🍴 ♥🥬🥬' -**@aly_carrington**

'In 2011, I took over a small restaurant in my town and shortly after, we turned it into a BBQ joint. Over the course of 5 years, I gained almost 150lbs. / 68kg. I weighed 348 lbs. / 158kg. I also developed severe joint pain and was taking 21 (4,200mg) ibuprofen daily. I had horrible sleep apnoea, and eventually was pre-diabetic, had high cholesterol, and high blood pressure. In 2016, I developed severe Edema. My hands, feet and legs were always swollen. I saw my doctor many times and the answer was always to throw pills at me. I was prescribed an anti-inflammatory, a pain killer, and a muscle relaxer. They seemed to help a little, but never fixed the issues and the Edema persisted. I even had a deep vein thrombosis scan and a couple of EKG's. I was never once talked to about my diet! Even being a fat guy. [..] In September 2016, I began having severe gastrointestinal pain. On October 3rd, 2016 I was hospitalized for it. They ran many tests, gave me NO answers, did not address my diet, and prescribed MORE medications. Upon release from the hospital, I had a conversation with my 68 year old extremely healthy, mostly plant based mom. Her words to me were "Don't fill those prescriptions, FOOD IS MEDICINE! Do the research!". So I did! I was unable to work and am an avid research junkie so I poured through the internet and medical journals for an anti-inflammatory diet.

Beginning Oct 5th, 2016 I stopped eating beef, pork, and chicken, and limited my dairy consumption to less than half of what I was eating, and stopped drinking soda. I included turmeric into my diet and started hydrating with lemon and lime in my water. I also limited my refined carbohydrate intake. In a little over 2 weeks, my Edema was gone and my blood pressure stabilized into the normal range. In 100 days, I lost 80lbs. / 36kg!!

In February 2017, I watched the documentary 'Forks Over Knives' and immediately stopped consuming cheese due to the Casein, Casomorphins, and IGF-1 in dairy (More info on that in my post "Giving Up Cheese & Going Vegan"). Within 3 weeks of ditching dairy, my lifelong struggle of daily anxiety magically disappeared. As I continued to research, I then gave up eggs and fish realizing that I had no need for this protein source in my diet, nor did I need the additional cholesterol. I have now been plant based for 1 year.

In November 2017, I had blood work done and everything is exceptional! I am currently at 200 lbs. / 90.7kg in 16 months. That is a 148lb. / 67kg weight loss!!!' **@respectfullivin**

The story above comes from a lovely man called Jeff! He has a blog and posts often so here is a link if you would like to hear some more - **https://www.arespectfullife.com/**

'I was diagnosed with polycystic ovary syndrome when I was 14 and all my doctors told me that if I wanted to lose weight and be able to have children later in my life I would need to up my meat intake and cut down on carbs. I blindly followed as a scared and uneducated child and started a low carb high fat diet. It made me feel terrible but I remembered what the doctor told me and I was losing a lot of weight. I made it somewhere where I felt okay with my weight and started eating carbs again and I gained it ALL back within 2 months. I redeveloped my eating disorder and started calorie restricting to 200 a day. Then one night, I stumbled on Earthlings on YouTube and- against all medical advice- I cut out animal products overnight. I was so disgusted. Veganism healed me! I got a handle on my weight in a sustainable way, I recovered my relationship with food, my reproductive health stabilized, and my-self-love increased more than anything. I came for the animals and the health benefits were more than I could have ever dreamed of!' -**@Cashwemilkstan**

'I first went vegetarian after choosing to do a mandatory school project on animal testing. I began learning a lot about other types of animal cruelty as I researched and started followed vegan/vegetarian social media accounts. I was a vegetarian for about nine months before transitioning into veganism. Through documentaries and social media, I realized that the dairy and egg industries are also extremely cruel to animals. It made sense to be a vegan: it's better for the animals, planet, and your health.' - **@collinrenfro**

'Well I guess I should start by saying that I am diagnosed with CFS (Chronic Fatigue Syndrome), EDS (Ehlers-Danlos Syndrome) and Fibromyalgia which are all chronic illnesses that started to surface when I was just 14. For years I had questioned veganism but it was only when I started to form disordered eating habits that I decided to take control and go vegan. This gave me a chance to control my disordered eating as I no longer had to live with the guilt of eating animals and I finally understood that I could thrive this way both nutritionally and ethically. I personally started by cutting out dairy. This was very easy for me as I have access to plenty of alternatives. My partner also had to cut out dairy due to allergies so it worked out well. Next was cutting out meat, I had stopped eating red meat 2 years prior and was only consuming chicken. Once I found alternatives to my meals I found it easier to cut out animal products and within 3 months I had converted my diet and lifestyle to being vegan. My partner followed me in this and also went vegan with me. I've learned so much about food, nutrition and cooking since becoming vegan.

I've now been vegan for 6 months and I won't ever go back. I do it for the animals, the environment and myself. I have personally seen a huge improvement in my physical and mental health since changing my diet to plant-based. I have more physical and mental energy, a better outlook on life and have way more "good" days with my chronic illnesses than I did before. These changes were an unexpected side effect. My partner has also felt benefits and we

always enjoy coming up with new recipes to try together.' -
@milkygamerguts

'My mom and my step dad own a farm where they have over 40 cows. My dad has hunted and fished his entire life and I used to fish with him, but I could never hunt. He had me shoot a squirrel one time when I was about 8 and it was a devastating experience for me. I cried and cried and said I'd never kill another animal. Fast forward 10 years when I'm 18 and living on my own. I started seeing vegan activism online and it was a perspective I had never heard before. I had never even met a vegetarian, let alone a vegan. When I discovered how horrible factory farming was, I vowed to only eat meat that was from my mom and step dad's farm. I still ate meat occasionally from other places but I was a picky eater and found it really hard to cut it out completely.

I travelled to Costa Rica later that year. At this point I was eating meat maybe once a week, but in Costa Rica due to the language barrier every time I ordered food it had meat on it, even when I tried to order without. I felt horrible and sick. I vowed to never eat meat again and I haven't since. Then for the next 6 months I worked on cutting out the rest of the animal products. Luckily my boyfriend was completely on board and working towards the same goals. We often said "I don't know if I can ever be 100% vegan" but we continued to watch YouTube videos about veganism and one day we were watching one about the link between cancer and cow's milk and we decided we had enough of the excuses and we were gonna go fully vegan.

I never expected to experience all of the health benefits I did. I used to get frequent UTIs (about 3-4 a year) and now I literally have not had one since going vegan nearly 2 years ago. I had baaad acne, now I usually get about 1 zit before my period starts and that's it. My periods used to last 7-9 days and I would cramp for 2-3 days. Now they usually last about 4-5 and I only have cramps for like half of a day. I was always a little chunky, but only in my stomach. When I cut out animal products I had a flat stomach for the first time in my life. I gain muscle much easier as a vegan. I get colds much less frequently and when I do get a cold i don't feel like I'm dying like I used to, and they last less time. I never get constipated or have diarrhoea. My allergies are practically non-existent now. My only regret is not going vegan sooner. 🐐' - **Susan**

'I grew up a fan of meat. I remember telling my mother I'm not a goat to eat grass (referring to spinach and the likes). I also grew up with bipolar disorder type II. After I woke up to a panic attack one morning after another messy, messy (I was addicted to SH for over 10 yrs.) suicide attempt, I started thinking of how I never want to feel that way again. Among my choice of recovery, I began seeking help through religion. I read and then studied the whole bible and nothing inside it gave me any empowerment of going on. I then began researching Islamic, Hindu, Jewish and African voodoo to which none got me convinced as an answer either.

Amongst my religions studies, I picked up a few practises from most such as meditation, dance/praise & worship as well as yoga. Along more research on yoga I came across plant based eating and intentional living and thought, like I grew up thinking "argh we're all gonna die though" until my very own intuition started asking me why I eat meat? I questioned my intent to it then decided to cut meat down and then out. After two weeks of that decision someone tweeted how The Happy Vegan by Russell Simmons changed their lives and I asked her where I could get it, she then forwarded the book to me and I, who thought I could not survive without toasted cheese, began to get revolted by anything from animals considered food/ingredients that I cleared my fridge and pantry out just a few pages within the book.

I did not expect to find so much clarity after cutting meat out years ago but the books clearly explained everything. It's been a year since I decided to not eat anything with animals, my compassion for living things has broadened a whole lot. I give thanks to plants every time I prepare my food for the fuel and nutrients that keep me going. I have more mental clarity, more energy, more animals that really seem to feel that I'm a vessel for love, more variety in the food I make [...] I've also influenced my parents to be more plant based and they tell me of how their health is getting better, my dad had feet inflammatory problems that has gone completely after cutting out meat. My partner has also become plant based and I'm literally watching his health get restored too. I had two breast lumps in 2014 and since being alkaline plant based in just two weeks I significantly only feel one small lump. It's changed my life SO much I'm sad there's such a negative stigma around the name "vegan". But its fear and guilt I can only keep hoping people rid themselves of any actually research. - **@geekjulieta**

'I was 13 and suffering with major digestive issues, stomach constantly swollen, insatiable hunger and the pain was indescribable. These issues couple with body dysmorphia from being called fat all my life pushed me to become vegetarian. My issues improved but my eating disorder did not. 2 years later in 2015 I decided to cut milk out of my diet, fearing that may be the cause. That lead me to revolutionising my diet and over the years I have converted into veganism. I regularly attend vegan festivals, have done since I was 15 and I've been vegan for two years now. At the start of this year I officially beat my eating disorder all thanks to a healthy diet that doesn't make me feel guilty.' - **@gingerbombharry**

'When Erin (a fellow vegan) and I first hung out she mentioned how she was vegan and I thought it was really cool but I also thought I could never do it because of the fact that I love cheese and meat and all of that stuff. Then one day I decided to be vegetarian for 1 month to see what it was like and at first it was difficult because they rest of my family are meat eaters and I have a large family. However, as time progressed and the more research and documentary's I watched about animal agriculture and the healthy benefits that come with a plant biased diet made me realize that I was doing the right things for the animals and for myself. I feel more happy and I've noticed significant health differences and honestly it is the coolest thing I have ever been a part of because now I am a part of a huge vegan family on twitter and they are so important, supportive and influential to me and I couldn't be more happier because of them.' - **@jxvieralarcon**

'Since a child, I had always been a huge fan of everything considered awful to vegans. Meat, cheese, milk- I adored the stuff. I was raised by parents, who also, didn't really understand the point of being vegan, as they themselves were raised to eat animal products ... it was considered the norm (and still is for most people). Cheese was probably my favourite food in the world, and I could live off creamy foods, milkshakes, you name it. I was also a fan of meat, I wouldn't say I was the biggest meat eater, but I'd happily eat a rare steak and absolutely loved chicken.

I had dabbled in vegetarianism during my teens, and once lasted nearly a year (I think this was around 2014), until it got to Christmas day and I gave in and ate meat. Since then, I just ate what I wanted, not thinking about it.

It wasn't until last year when I noticed a difference in my body. I remember working in my office job around July time and feeling so rubbish all the time. Every single day my stomach would bloat, so much that my own mom would say I looked pregnant (I'm like a size 6/8, so you can imagine how big I would bloat!). By morning I was fine, and my stomach was back to being flat. Then it would come to afternoon time and I would balloon. I tried everything, from eating boring salads for my lunch, to eating less food altogether, and I even gave up caffeine, just to try and find the cause of the issue. I even had an ultrasound scan to look for any problems, and she just said my bowels were 'compacted' (sorry for the TMI ha-ha!).

After eating healthy, reducing my salt and sugar intake, and upping my water intake, nothing worked. I then did some research online and read that dairy can be a cause of bloating. Fine, I thought, I'll give it a go!

I stopped eating cheese and milk around this time, instead opting for soya milk in my tea (which I took to really easily), and avoiding cheese at all costs. I still allowed myself to eat products which contained milk in the ingredients for a while, as I wasn't vegan at that point. Cheese was a little harder. Like I said, cheese was one of my favourite foods in the world, but I persevered for my health.

After just a couple of weeks, I noticed a huge change in my body- this time for good! The bloating vanished, and I generally felt a lot better in myself. If I'm honest, I didn't find giving up dairy that hard. I mean, at the end of the day it's just food and it's something I could live without.

At the start of September, I went on holiday with my family and my boyfriend to Spain. My boyfriend also gave up milk- he doesn't eat cheese at all anyway but decided to switch to soya after I told him how much better I felt. Luckily, the local supermarket down the road sold soya milk- so I managed to go dairy free whilst on holiday too! Well, most of the time- I do recall having a couple pizzas whilst dining out, and some ice creams. I found it pretty easy being in Spain, as we were self-catered so could control what we ate more than if we stayed somewhere all-inclusive.

I can't quite remember how long it had been since I got back from holiday, I think a week or so, but I decided to watch Cowspiracy and What The Health one evening in bed. Right there and then, I decided to remove animal products from my diet completely. As in, I woke up the next morning, and I went vegan. Looking back this did seem pretty drastic, as I was still eating meat and products with milk in them just the day before. However, I think the fact I had stopped drinking milk in itself and had already reduced my intake of dairy, I wasn't worried.

I questioned myself why I hadn't gone vegan sooner. I mean, I've loved animals since I was a child, but my brain never made the connection. Now I know more about what goes on in the dairy and meat industry, I will never consume it again. I also went vegan not just for the animals, but for my health in general as the more I learned about animal products, the more they seemed extremely bad for our health. Also, the impact the industries have on the environment shocked me really badly and I wish more people spoke about this as I seemed clueless to most of the facts.

Obviously, this did prove challenging at first, especially as my kitchen cupboards weren't exactly prepared! I remember having to go to work the next few days and having to buy my lunch out. This did prove difficult. I worked in the Jewellery Quarter in Birmingham, and if you know the area, you know food there isn't cheap for someone on a budget. I would usually head to the cheapest cafe 5 minutes down the road as you walk into the city centre, and grab myself a toasted Panini or baguette. Of course, that day I became vegan I walked in there and took one look at the menu and walked straight out as they had no options at all. Me and my friend at work would always grab lunch together, and I remember that day she spent about 15 minutes with me walking around trying to find something for me to eat, thank god for her patience! In the end, I had to go to the most expensive cafe right near my work and was so happy to discover they had plenty of vegan options, including salads and sandwiches. However, this wasn't affordable to do every day, so I did go for a big food shop at the end of the week and stock up on vegan-friendly food so I could take my own lunch!

Now, It's now 2018, a whole year later, and I feel better than ever. My bloating has gone, my skin has cleared up, and my nails and hair feel fab. My mood is also a lot better, and my hormonal mood swings seem less severe! I've learnt more recipes and done more cooking and baking than ever before- and LOVE every second of it. I will never go back!' - **@EmmaPowellArt**

'I had never heard of vegans, only vegetarians and I thought they were crazy bc I used to think we -needed- meat. But I've always been against animal testing and fur. So I started wearing cruelty free makeup and that opened the doors to a lot of information. I was reading about the dairy industry when something clicked in my brain and I realized what I was doing. I've always loved animals so much and I couldn't keep contributing to their suffering. So I basically went vegan overnight. I still ate dairy and eggs when I was out with family and friends for about 3 months because I wanted to avoid confrontation. So it took me a bit to get all the answers I needed about veganism and to find support online of other vegans to feel comfortable enough saying "no" to others when I was out. I've been vegan for about three years now and my only regret is not having gone vegan sooner. ♥🐾' - Foxxy Fay

As you can tell, people come to veganism from all different places with different personal experiences, reasons, results and progress! Nobody goes vegan the same way and that is why however your journey goes it is important to remember that it is still valid. If you go vegan overnight or if it takes you a bit of time, all that matters is that you are trying and you are doing more than you were before!

Food & Diet

So, now we are all feeling inspired. We also have our knowledge, or we at least know where to go to get it and we have our everyday stories that remind us that anyone can go vegan. I'm now going to help you make this an even more probable reality as we are going to delve in to the big scary part of veganism. The diet. When people think of veganism they think of giving up their bacon and their cheese and they get a little bit stressed out by it all! So, naturally, this is what we are going to face first. When people first transition into veganism it can be scary as you don't know what your doing, where you should go or how you should go about it. In this section I'll do my best to address every area of food and diet you may be stuck on!

Part One - My Top Five Tips

Whether you are taking this journey from being a meat eater, vegetarian, or someone who is already making steps towards being fully vegan, this is the bit you will want to take on board before you begin. If you feel like you've read this before, you may well have as I am taking it from my very own blog. These tips may seem very basic and obvious to some of you but remember that you have to start somewhere. It is a much easier journey when you take it one step at a time and take each of these suggestions on board.

1) Add before you subtract

Add foods into your diet before you start taking out animal products! Simple as can be! Find the replacements you'll enjoy so when you remove the animal products you can swap things out immediately. When you have foods sitting there ready to replace the meat, dairy or eggs that you are used to it feels that much easier to let them go.

2) Don't be afraid to try new things

Some vegan replacements are awful. There is no denying it, there are some however that are amazing – taste, look and feel like the real thing. Don't be put off if you happen to encounter a bad thing first! The replacement market is growing by the day and you'll be able to find the perfect replacement for you out there somewhere!

3) Don't let slip ups stop you!

Everyone slips up from time to time, it's only human. If you find you have a burger when you're transitioning or accidentally eat something with milk in, **it is ok**!! The important thing is that you keep going! Your health, the animals and the planet will thank you for even trying! Going vegan is not like a diet, if you slip up, you haven't ruined the whole day of eating. Take it in your stride and carry on with the vegan lifestyle that you are adapting too.

4) Educate yourself

Do your research! Whether that be through documentaries, studies or talking to fellow vegans! Knowledge will always help you reinforce your moral choices. It will also reaffirm to you why you are living the way you chose to live through veganism!

5) Shop cheap

Places like Aldi and Lidl are fantastic for cheap fruit, veggies, grains and pulses! They also have loads of accidentally vegan products (I promise label reading gets easier) so shop there where you can. Fruit and veg stalls also offer great deals on in season veg, which often keeps well in the freezer, and will save you loads of money (and plastic).

So how are we feeling? Are you still with me? If you are starting to feel overwhelmed, put this guide down for a minute and come back to it when you are feeling less intimidating! I'll still be here when you are ready! It can be a lot to take in when you are making a complete lifestyle change, so don't let anything scare you into doing things at a pace you are not comfortable with! Remember this is your personal journey, and the more time you take the easier it will feel.

Part Two - Vegan and Non-Vegan Alcohol

That's right, they have even found a way to make some alcohol non-vegan, just when you thought it was safe. You'll find that a lot of the spirits are fine to drink but some of the beers, ciders and wines however aren't! Below I'm going to list *some* of the most popular **vegan** alcohols. If your favourite drink isn't on this list give it a check whether that be on the internet or through contacting the company directly! I would search it and check to be 100% sure! It is also important to note that this is a UK based list and you might find variants from country to country.

Unless stated this list includes original flavours only (some other flavours may also be vegan friendly but if it isn't all of them I won't be listing the others!).

Vegan Beers, Lagers & Ciders

Beck's

Budweiser

Bulmers

Carlsberg

Corona

Heineken

San Miguel

Stella Artois

Brothers Cider

Old Mout

Bud Light

Peroni

Sol

Estrella Galicia (gluten free)

Thatcher's Gold

Aspalls Suffolk Cyder

Angry Orchard

Vodka, Whiskey, Gin, Rum & Liquors

Absolut (All flavours)

Bacardi

Bell's

The Famous Grouse

Haig Club Clubman

Smirnoff

Pimms

Jagermeister

Jim Beam

Captain Morgan Rum

Jack Daniels

Don Julio Tequila

Jose Cuervo Especial Tequila

Jose Cuervo

Gin Fizz

Gordon's Pink Gin

Malibu

Southern Comfort

Volaire Blue Curaçao

Ales

Guinness

Ruddles

I have not included wines and cocktails on this list as it varies vastly from place to place due to things such as own brand products and who/where the drink is made! I hope this helps with the actual process of buying your drinks whether it's on a night out or having a relaxed evening at home.

Part Three - Eating Out

Now we have our drinks ready we should dive into the food! This section is dedicated to eating out. That's right, we are facing the big guns now. The dreaded 'what do I eat when I go out as a vegan??' well, as you are about to see, it is not as hard as you think. A lot of places have vegan options or vegetarian options where you just ask for no cheese. Below is a list of *some* of the places with vegan foods.

Just a reminder that this is a UK based section, although a lot of these should transfer to other countries I cannot guarantee that as a fact

Zizzi's

Pizza Hut

Nandos

Las Iguanas

Prezzo

Harvester

Pizza Express

Wagamama's

Wetherspoons

Toby Carvery

Yo! Sushi

The Real Greek

Pret A Manger

ASK Italian

Itsu

Giraffe

Leon

Byron Burgers

Carluccio's

Firezza

Bella Italia

Chiquito

Chimichanga

Taco Bell

Café Rouge

Frankie and Benny's

Starbucks

Greggs

And... I think that puts the rumour that it is impossible to eat out as a vegan to rest. As you can see, that just by this list of *some* restaurants that do vegan options, it is not as hard as it once was, or as you probably thought. Sometimes foods do need a little bit of adapting, but out of this list a lot of them do have pre-set vegan/veggie menus (which is very handy because then you do not have to search for the little V or Ve).

Part Four - Facing the Supermarkets

Okay, so now you can see that going out for food is not as hard as you thought it was, but then you must face the idea of cooking your own foods. This bit is the intimidating bit. If you have no idea, or no experience with 'vegan food' you tend to forget that you've cooked most of it before. You know how to cook your pasta, your veggies and your beans and legumes ... but you don't know how to fill a plate without the meat and dairy, right? Although this can be intimidating it can also be the fun part. As most people say they learnt how to cook when they went vegan (me being one of them) because they learned how to season properly, how to make big portions with foods they've always ate, but never seen as a 'central' part to a meal. This sounds like a lot to adapt to, right? Well, do not fear, I've already set you up with some lovely websites that will have some nice easy meals for you to play around with and you can of course play around with making your own recipes from scratch! In this section we are going to address every concern you may have about facing the stores for food. Whether that be what to buy, how to read the labels, how to lower the cost of your expenditures, what milks and fake meats to buy and so on and so forth!

Part Five - How to read the Labels

So I am going to walk you through it. You have made it to the store. You are ready to shop… but, wait a minute, you don't know how to read the labels. Do not fear my friend, in this little section I shall explain to you exactly what you are looking for.

On some occasions you are blessed to have items that simply have vegan on it such as the

Figure 2 http://veganblogger.com/vegan-product-labels.html (Accessed 14/06/18)

Figure 3 http://www.vegansouls.com/vegan-certification-on-food-labels (Accessed 14/06/18)

following;

Other times, they won't give it to you as clear as day.

Some products may be labelled as vegetarian and are in fact 'accidentally vegan', this is when you need to have a nosey around the full list of ingredients on the back. Things like dairy, dairy by-products and eggs will be put in bold on the packaging as these things are classed as 'common allergens' where as things like honey and beeswax are more often then not left out.

The first thing I would go about doing when I've picked up a vegetarian item, is look straight at the bolds. This is the quickest identifier of something non-vegan so train yourself to look at the bolds before anything else, instead of wasting your time and then seeing the second to last ingredient is something that you choose not to eat. Once the bolds are safe, have a look for other things like beeswax and honey. You'll find a bit deeper in the book that I have a list of *sneaky* non-vegan products that most of us forget or simply don't know about!

Part Six - Shopping List

Here I am going to break it down simply what I think is a good shopping list to start with! You can find a lot of vegan shopping lists online so if this one is not one that appeals to you search for vegan shopping lists and see what else you can find.

This is a shopping list that I would recommend as a basic place to start, it is not a strict guide, but it is one that I find very helpful and almost perfect for the foods I eat and the diet I follow. I follow a very high carb low fat diet, so this will show in this shopping list, but please remember this is just a guide, you can adapt to things however you want. In the interest of personal taste and adaptation, I will keep things like replacement meats, replacement cheeses and replacement milks off the list. I would recommend that you explore these on your own and find the ones that you personally like! This will be a shopping list for your initial move to veganism, so some of the foods on there will last longer than a week as they are staples to the diet! Once again, if you want some help with these things I will leave my twitter, Instagram, Facebook and email at the end of this guide and you can message me for some more personal advice! I would also recommend when you look around your supermarket to look for 'accidentally vegan foods' a lot of things that are like chicken noodles, bacon flavoured crisps or rice's are actually vegan!

This list will show you my basic staples and as you venture into the world of vegan meals, junk foods and accidentally vegan products you might find that you move on to bigger and better things! Either way this list is where *I* personally started out at.

This is the shopping list I *personally* would recommend!

Staples	Weekly	Seasonings

Pasta	Bananas	Salt
Rice	Apples	Pepper
Spaghetti	Oranges	Basil
Potatoes	Pears	Cumin
Sweet Potatoes	Bagels	Turmeric
Baked Beans	Tortilla Wraps	Cayenne Pepper
Red Kidney Beans	Seeded Loaf	Paprika
Pinto Beans	Courgettes	Parsley
Black Beans	Mushrooms	Garlic powder
Lentils	Peppers	Onion powder
Peanut Butter	Spinach	Curry Powder
Jam	Kale	Peri-Peri Seasoning
Maple Syrup	Avocado	Cinnamon
Brown Sugar	Baby Sweetcorn	Ginger
Frozen Peas	Lettuce	Sriracha Sauce
Frozen Sweetcorn	Hummus	Tabasco Sauce
Frozen Broccoli	Almonds	Vinaigrettes
Frozen Cauliflower		
Olive oil		
Nutritional Yeast		

This list is quite a juicy one, and that is without your meat, milks and cheese replacements. You will more than likely find you have a lot of these things in your diet already, or you might have slight variations regarding the fruits, veggies, and grains. We all have personal preferences when it comes to foods and our shopping list will fit those needs. While you transition into veganism you will find that you try new foods and new combos and you'll gradually settle into habits that you find suit you best. I live a very low-cost life, as I am a student, which means my shopping list revolves around the foods I can get for 50p in Aldi. As everything, we all have different budgets and different ideas on what we like to eat! I very rarely eat vegan cheeses or meat replacements, but I know others who live off them! It is all down to personal taste.

Part Seven - Milk & Meat Replacements

I unfortunately can't go into too much detail here as what I find readily available in supermarkets you may not. What I can do, is list common replacements, so things you will easily find replacements for or the types of replacements you might stumble upon. As you may or may not know, there are replacements for almost every meat product and there are loads of different milk replacements, so I will pop another list here (I promise these lists are not the whole book I know it is starting to feel that way). My first list will be the different types of milks you can try, these vary in price range and you might find that some types are better suited for different things. Personally, I use soya milk for everything, it's cheap and easy so I stick loyally by soya's side. This list will show you your options so if you don't find yourself getting along with one you can give another one a whirl.

No need to act like a baby cow anymore

Soya (sweetened or unsweetened)

Almond (sweetened or unsweetened)

Cashew

Hazelnut

Oat

Rice

Hemp

Flax

Coconut

Just a note that lactofree milk is normally NOT vegan

There are loads of different milks with loads of different price ranges, so it is up to you how you explore these. I personally would say try the cheapest ones you can see first just so you don't find yourself developing an 'expensive taste' as far as milk goes. You can find some of these for under 50p and some go to nearly £2 a bottle (as for everywhere else in the world I can't comment).

As promised we have list number two of our replacements, the types of meats you can replace. Lots of supermarkets have cheap own brand vegan meat replacements, some take a little bit of ingredient reading but a lot are labelled as vegan now. Common meat replacements are Linda McCartney, Quorn, Gardein, Frys and tofurkey.

Some of the most commonly meat replacements

Chicken nuggets

Sausages/ Mini sausages

Bacon

Burgers

Spicy burgers

Chicken pieces

Sausage rolls

Mince

Chicken strips

Fish fingers

Plain fillets

Breadcrumb covered fillets

Meatballs

There are meat replacements for almost all meats and even fish products, but some are a lot harder to find and a lot less likely to be on offer or in your local supermarket. These are the few that I find with ease, so if I am going to eat a meat replacement, these are the ones I find myself often reaching for.

Just a note regarding vegan cheese and butters – there are vegan cheeses for almost all types of cheese (including mozzarella, cream cheese and what I call 'Christmas cheeses' aka fancier cheeses). You will also find replacements for butter in things like; vitalite, olive spread, avocado spread, sunflower spread etc.

Part Eight - Shopping for Cheaper

Shop Seasonal

Seasonal fruit and veg is normally a lot cheaper to produce and therefore is sold off for a much lower a price! Below you'll find a list of what fruit and veg is in season in which months, I will also link my source, so you can check it out in more depth yourself! This may differ from country to country, but they are all easily found online so give your country a search and stick it on your fridge! If you need help finding yours, as standard, pop me a message!

Fruit and Veg Markets

Another way to get this fruit and veg cheap is to check at your local fruit and veg markets (this applies worldwide not just the UK!). Local produce can cost a lot less money and most places do 'bowls of veg' where you can buy a load of one item for £1. Once I got 6 avocados for £1 and three mangos for £1, so it is worth investigating your local markets!

Zero Waste Stores

If you have your own jars and containers already you might find that shopping in zero waste stores will save you some money! This varies from place to place but a lot of these zero waste stores sell their products cheaper as they are not having to cover the costs of packaging! This is also a good way to also reduce your plastic usage.

Bulk Buy Grains

You can often save money by buying your grains; pasta, rice, quinoa and couscous in bulk. As you are buying more you will find that a lot of the time they have a lower price. If you have the space for this I would recommend that you do this to save you a little bit more!

Read the price labels!

In a lot of supermarkets, you'll find the price labels have the main price and then how much the item works out as per kilo or per gram.

Heinz squeezy tomato ketchup 1.35kg
£2.99
22.1p per 100g

14·3355343·2·2·6

hellmanns squeezy ketchup 430ml
£1.57
36.5p per 100ml

14·7266974·3·3·12

Figure 4 http://www.thisismoney.co.uk/money/bills/article-2199154/Confusing-supermarket-pricing-misleads-consumers.html (Accessed 30/05/18)

As you can see, if you read the small print you will be able to see which item works out cheapest in the long run. This saves you from trying to do the maths yourself, and helps you work out if sometimes paying the extra is more beneficial.

Meal Prep/planning

Sit down on a Sunday evening, or a Tuesday morning or whenever it may be that you are free, and plan what you are going to eat for the next week for every meal and every snack (if you have that kind of willpower). This means you will be able to go into your cupboards, see what you have and what you don't, and write a list accordingly. Planning is key.

Non-branded foods

Don't be scared to try own brands or brand less foods, some of them taste identical to the brands! Non-branded foods are normally half the price, with half the chemicals and the same taste!

Grow your own

If you are feeling brave, try growing your own fruits and veg! Tomatoes, strawberries, green beans, apples, cucumbers and potatoes are things we grow at home every year!

Part Nine - Seasonal Fruit & Veg

Another way to make your shopping cheaper is by shopping in season.

January; Apples, Beetroot, Brussels Sprouts, Cabbage, Carrots, Celery, Kale, Leeks, Mushrooms, Onions, Parsnips, Pears, Spring Onions, Squash, Swedes, Turnips.

February; Apples, Beetroot, Brussels Sprouts, Cabbage, Carrots, Kale, Leeks, Mushrooms, Onions, Parsnips, Pears, Spring Onions, Squash, Swedes.

March; Artichoke, Beetroot, Cabbage, Carrots, Cucumber, Leeks, Parsnip, Purple Sprouting Broccoli, Radishes, Rhubarb, Spring Onions, Watercress.

April; Artichoke, Beetroot, Cabbage, Carrots, New Potatoes, Kale, Morel Mushrooms, Parsnips, Radishes, Rhubarb, Rocket, Spinach, Spring Greens, Spring Onions, Watercress.

May; Artichoke, Asparagus, Aubergine, Beetroot, Chillies, Elderflowers, Lettuce, New Potatoes, Peas, Peppers, Radishes, Rhubarb, Spinach, Spring Greens, Spring Onions, Strawberries, Watercress.

June; Asparagus, Aubergine, Beetroot, Blackcurrants, Broad Beans, Broccoli, Cauliflower, Cherries, Chillies, Courgettes, Cucumber, Elderflowers, Gooseberries, Lettuce, New Potatoes, Peas, Peppers, Radishes, Raspberries, Redcurrants, Rhubarb, Runner Beans, Spring Greens, Spring Onions, Strawberries, Summer Squash, Swiss Chard, Turnips, Watercress.

July; Aubergine, Beetroot, Blackberries, Blackcurrants, Blueberries, Broad Beans, Broccoli, Carrots, Cauliflower, Cherries, Chillies, Courgettes, Cucumber, Gooseberries, French Beans, Garlic, New Potatoes, Onions, Peas, Potatoes, Radishes, Raspberries, Redcurrants, Rhubarb, Runner Beans, Samphire, Spring Greens, Spring Onions, Strawberries, Summer Squash, Swish Chard, Tomatoes, Turnips, Watercress.

August; Aubergine, Beetroot, Blackberries, Blackcurrants, Broad Beans, Broccoli, Carrots, Cauliflower, Cherries, Chillies, Courgettes, Cucumber, French Beans, Garlic, Greengages, Leeks, Lettuce, Mangetout, Marrow, Mushrooms, Parsnips, Peas, Peppers, Potatoes, Plums, Pumpkin, Radishes, Raspberries, Redcurrants,

Rhubarb, Runner Beans, Spring Greens, Spring Onions, Strawberries, Summer Squash, Sweetcorn, Swiss Chard, Tomatoes, Watercress.

September; Aubergine, Beetroot, Blackberries, Broccoli, Brussels Sprouts, Butternut Squash, Carrots, Cauliflower, Celery, Courgettes, Chillies, Cucumber, Garlic, Kale, Leeks, Lettuce, Mangetout, Marrow, Onions, Parsnips, Pears, Peas, Peppers, Plums, Potatoes, Pumpkin, Radishes, Raspberries, Rhubarb, Runner Beans, Spinach, Spring Onions, Strawberries, Summer Squash, Sweetcorn, Swiss Chard, Tomatoes, Turnips, Watercress, Wild Mushrooms.

October; Aubergine, Apples, Beetroot, Blackberries, Broccoli, Brussels Sprouts, Butternut Squash, Carrots, Cauliflower, Celery, Chestnuts, Chillies, Courgette, Cucumber, Elderberries, Kale, Leeks, Lettuce, Onions, Parsnips, Pears, Peas, Potatoes, Pumpkin, Radishes, Runner Beans, Spinach, Spring Greens, Spring Onions, Summer Squash, Swede, Sweetcorn, Tomatoes, Turnips, Watercress, Wild Mushrooms, Winter Squash.

November; Apples, Beetroot, Brussels Sprouts, Butternut Squash, Cabbage, Carrots, Cauliflower, Celeriac, Celery, Chestnuts, Cranberries, Elderberries, Kale, Leeks, Onions, Parsnips, Pears, Potatoes, Pumpkin, Swede, Swiss Chard, Turnips, Watercress, Wild Mushrooms, Winter Squash.

December; Apples, Beetroot, Brussels Sprouts, Carrots, Celeriac, Celery, Chestnuts, Cranberries, Kale, Leeks, Mushrooms, Onions,

Parsnips, Pears, Potatoes, Pumpkin, Red Cabbage, Swede, Swiss Chard, Turnips, Watercress, Winter Squash.[24]

Now that is a list, if I've ever seen one! This lovely list is courtesy of Vegsoc.com and there are even more online! Remember that this is UK based so this list will vary from country to country!

Part Ten- Making New Meals

We've got our list and we have our places to go when we are too lazy to cook, but we have not faced the idea of actually getting into our kitchen and cooking. Well, for the average human, you still must cook at home, whether you want to or not. Everyone likes different foods, meals and types of flares in their cooking, so I will not be including recipes (this time round).

I know it can be scary when your swapping foods you are used to for foods you have had zero experience in and you are not quite sure if you are even going to enjoy them or if they are going to go straight in the bin. Have no fear, this is how we all become the pro chefs that we are... well, some people never get to be pro chef, they find out all but one pot noodles are vegan, that most super noodles are vegan, and a fast amount of crisps, biscuits and sweets are and that kitchen fades back into the back of their mind like it always was. I'm not here to judge, so if that's how you want to live you go for it. This section may not be for you, unless you want to lie to yourself and say that you're changing everything

---

[24] https://www.vegsoc.org/sslpage.aspx?pid=525 (Accessed 30/05/18)

about your living and you are going to start cooking and doing yoga and meditating for an hour a day, or whatever that lie may be. The kitchen is a scary place for anyone, just remember, as a vegan, there is less chance that your undercooked or overcooked food will kill you or make you ill (and yes that is a valid excuse to take your food out the oven early because you are hungry).

Tip #1 – transition into making vegan foods

If there is one thing you are going to have drilled into your brain by the end of this guide, it is that I 100% support and believe that you should transition into every aspect of veganism. I'd suggest trying to make 2-4 vegan meals a week for your first month or so of transitioning. If you eat your three meals a day making four out of twenty-one meals vegan, is not very intimidating at all. I would also recommend in your first week or two of transitioning you focus on removing the obviously non-vegan foods like cheese, milk and meats. As you get more comfortable start look at ingredients lists and swap them out as slowly or quickly as you feel comfortable with!

Tip #2 – try new meals

Out of these 2-4 meals that you are trying to make weekly, try to make at least one of them a new recipe, a new type of food or just different to your normal eating style/habits. In doing this you are making your dietary horizons much broader. You do not want to limit your foods, you want to create as many options for yourself as possible. You are already running around the kitchen like a headless chicken, why not throw in a meal that you have no knowledge about into the mix as well?

Tip #3 - find different vegan recipes for your favourite meals

There are vegan recipes out there for every meal. Whether your favourite food is pizza, buffalo wings, mac N cheese or fish and chips, there are multiple vegan versions out there. Try as many different recipes as you can until you find the one that feels right for you! I promise that you will be able to make your favourite meals vegan (there is even vegan ribs out there). Don't be afraid to find a recipe and play around with it until you find it's to your taste! You are freer in the kitchen than you may have ever been.

Tip #4 - try a new meat/cheese replacement weekly

Meat replacements are something that you have to play around with until you find the ones that work for you. There are so many brands of meat replacements out there, it is as plain as going around them until you find the ones that you find the best! Everyone wants different things from their foods and everyone has different brand preferences, you will find yours if you keep an open mind and you keep your willing to try!

Tip #5 – have fun with your foods!

Nobody is expecting you to whip up fine cuisine every meal. Some meals are burnt, some are sloppy, some are terribly undercooked, and others are just terrible. As someone who posts pictures of their food on the internet, I can 100% vouch for you when I say just go with whatever you think might work! If the meal is a mess but tastes good who actually cares? Enjoy what you are making and see where freedom with your food can take you! Just be warned, not everything you do with an open mind will taste as delicious as I'm sure you hope it will!

Tip #6 – you don't have to be a vegan health God

I think the title of this one explains it all... you don't have to make every meal as green as possible, just make foods that you like and foods that you would want to eat. Don't make yourself miserable.

Tip #7 – Meal Prepping

Meal prepping is a brilliant way to save time in the kitchen and getting good foods in your belly! Things like chilis and curries can be made in bulk and frozen! You can even freeze some vegan sauces and some vegan meat replacements that have been cooked. If you make a couple of days' worth of meals one evening it will save you from having to debate what you are going to cook in the evening when you want to relax. I know this applies to every diet you follow, but when you are trying to make completely new foods on the weekly or even daily basis have some premade will be like a weight off your shoulders (and may even help you quickly find your favourites!).

Tip #8 – Utensils

These are not essentials for the vegan diet. These are things that someone who likes pasta dishes, potato dishes, chillies and curries (me) find very handy to own. You can get some of these things reasonably priced (again ask me and I'll direct you to the right places) and they'll arrive quickly! I would recommend getting your hands on the following;

A rice cooker

A blender

An air fryer

A good Wok

A load of reusable Tupperware (that can freeze)

A reusable water bottle

You might not find yourself needing all of these or even any, but I would recommend them for someone who is going to make a lot of their own foods, and foods in bulk! I would suggest you have a look at some recipes and pin them to your bookmarks bar, fold over pages or whatever it may be and see how many of them suggest having these things. Blenders saved my life when it came to have mac N cheese or avocado pasta and the air fryer enables me to make my own chips, wedges or roast potatoes without a load of oil! It is all down to personal preference and what *you* want to be making! So, don't worry if you can't afford these things or don't think you will use them!

(A reusable water bottle however is essential because save the planet and keep plastic out the ocean ok?)

Part Eleven - Nutrients in Fruit & Veg

A serious note about food

My final bit of advice regarding your meals is not a tip it's something that is quite factual. That's right, serious Amy is here to give you a serious talk about the seriousness of food. You are going to want to make your portions bigger than you are used to. A lot of people go vegan, try to live of salad, and get no way near the right amounts of calories or nutrients. If counting calories is a safe place for you, I would recommend for the first couple of weeks you use apps that allow you to see what you are eating and what nutrients you are getting. If counting calories *isn't* a safe space for you, please be careful with how you eat and do not put this lifestyle before your health. Your health is the single most important thing when it comes to lifestyle choices so please be careful not to strain yourself or do anything damaging. It is 1000% possible for you to go vegan if you have suffered with issues surrounding foods and I do not want you to feel dishearten by hearing this, you must make sure you are not fuelling a fire within your transition. A lot of people successfully go vegan without encouraging negative disorders or patterns within their eating, but that does not mean it is a safe place for everyone. Remember there are doctors, dieticians, nutritionists or just regular people like you and me who can help you with this journey, as I've said a thousand times feel free to email or message me and I will gladly send you in the direction of someone who can help you through this with one to one support and advice. Remember you are stronger than everything you have suffered through and that you will be able to over come whatever is trying to hold you back.

How to avoid dying of a protein deficiency

The hot topic when it comes to vegan is currently and probably always will be based around nutrients and supplements. Most of this fear was purposely generated by the meat and dairy industry to keep people eating their products and making them money, in other cases its just word of mouth. For example, nobody cares or even knows what B12 is, until you tell them you are a vegan. But, the worry is very real and present, so I have listened some good foods for; protein, calcium, iron, Omega 3 fatty acids and vitamin D.

Protein

Lentils, black beans, broccoli, hemp seeds, chia seeds, tofu, peanut butter and potatoes.

Iron

Soy beans, porridge, rice, quinoa, pumpkin seeds, chickpeas and red kidney beans.

Calcium

Broccoli, almonds, tahini, kale and collard greens.

Omega 3 Fatty Acids

Flax seeds, hemp seeds, walnuts and Brussel sprouts.

Vitamin D

Mushrooms, fortified soy milks, tofu or pop yourself in the sun for half an hour or so.

B12

Fortified milks, cereals or nutritional yeast (when it comes to B12 please make sure you take into consideration that most meat/dairy animals consume their B12 through fortified means).

There are loads of facts and suggestions online for almost every nutrient or supplement you may find yourself worrying about. The facts in this little list are provided to you courtesy of Peta[25]. It is as easy as having a little google for yourself for you to check these things, but as you can see, there are ways to get these nutrients that a lot of people find themselves worry about.

Non-vegan Chemicals

This is another thing I would only suggest looking into once you have found your footing in the basic areas of veganism! A lot of the time chemicals or artificial ingredients are added into your food without you having any idea what they are! And, unfortunately for us vegans, a few of these are meat or contain animal products. Below is a list of the chemicals/artificial ingredients that you should try to avoid! Remember everybody slips up, and sometimes you may forget to look at that is ok you are only human after all!

Additives such as; E120, E322, E422, E 471, E542, E631, E901 and E904 can be nonvegan.

Cochineal/carmine comes from ground insect scales.

Gelatine is a thickening agent often from the bone of pigs.

---

[25] https://www.peta.org/issues/animals-used-for-food/essential-nutrients/ (Accessed 29/05/18)

Isinglass is like gelatine, but is from fish bladder and can be found in beers and wines.

Omega-3 Fatty Acids is often from fish but there are vegan alternatives.

Shellac is from a female insect and often is used as a glaze for sweets.

Vitamin D3 often derived from fish oil.

L. Cysteine an ingredient often sourced from feathers (but sometimes human hair?).

Whey a milk product.

These are the products you may bump into regularly, try and keep your eye out for them! The list of non-vegan chemicals grows almost by the day, so keep yourself up-to-date with these things! This list shows you some of the *most* common ones!

Now You're stressed right?

So that is most of food tackled for you! You'll find you'll learn more and more as you grow through your journey to veganism! Do not fear if you are finding yourself stressed or worried about all these new things to look out for or think about, you can take as much time as you need! The chances are you are going to slip up, one way or another and that is completely fine and normal. It's all a part of the process. The most important thing is that you are trying your best and you are willing to adapt and make these changes in your life. Please take your time in your transition as if you overwhelm yourself you are more likely to give up or put everything on pause. Remind yourself why you are doing this and take it one step at a time.

Beauty & Hygiene

Well done!! You've officially made it through the first section of this guide. You've tackled the main bits and pieces that go towards eating vegan. Don't worry if you are still a bit unsteady or if you have questions, later in the guide there is a full-blown Q&A type of section where I'll be giving you my best average vegan advice. This section here is one that people often struggle with. Once you've got the food down, you tend to start analysing everything in your life. Looking at your hair products, make up, skin care, shower gel, bath bombs and the rest.

Within this section of the book I will try and address as many areas of beauty and hygiene as I can! This is quite a broad area, so items I may be discussing that I use, you might not and vice versa. Hopefully I will be able to provide you with enough brands that you can safely shop in every area of health and beauty! The idea of looking at all your beauty and hygiene items might be intimidating at first, just remember, as I've said many times, take your time and work things in and out of your life at a pace that is comfortable for you.
(New drinking game, drink every time I tell you to take your time with your transition).

This area can be tricky because some companies sell their products to contain 'vegan formulas' but they are companies that use animal testing or sell in china (china requires animal testing on their products by law). A quick way to check this is to check for the leaping bunny logo or an anti-animal testing logo (see below).

The 'leaping bunny' is an internationally recognised symbol that identifies a product as cruelty free, and is normally the safest thing to look on a product to know it is vegan.

Part One - Top Tips

Tip #1 Look for the leaping bunny

As above mentioned, look for this little guy! With a lot of big companies throwing around the word 'vegan' when it comes to their recipes, a lot of people accidentally support cruelty. If you see this guy it is **cruelty free**. The leaping bunny is a sure sign of whether or not animals have been used before you have even addressed the formula of your product! Make sure he is one of the first things you look for when you are looking at a beauty or hygiene product!

Tip #2 Look for the word vegan

A lot of companies now label on their products if it is safe for vegans or not. This is obviously a quick way for you to check your being safe with your products! Superdrug for example is excellent at showing whether their own brand products are vegan or not!

Tip #3 Your tools

Check where your make up brushes, tooth brush and hairbrush come from! Sometimes they manage to sneak animal products into these things without any sort of indication at all. Swap these products out in your own way or at your own pace! When I've asked my fellow vegans about their transitioning with beauty products, their brushes etc seems to be the thing that they most commonly forget about!

Tip #4 Use apps

If you find yourself struggling with the confusing ingredient lists just download an app to do it for you! Most of these scan products and will come back to you in seconds about whether it is safe for you to use! Some of these apps include the following; Bunnyfree, Cruelty-Free, Choose Cruelty Free and Animal-Free.

Tip #5 Go through your old products

Now, how you face your old products is your own personal decision! Some people keep them as they bought them before they went vegan, some people give them away and some people just bin them! That is your choice. What you *should* do is check which of your products are safe and which aren't! Then you know where you need to make some changes and where you are safe.

Part Two - Make Up

There are lots of debates when it comes to what make up brands are vegan and what brands are not. There are some companies that are technically vegan, but their parent company is not, or there are select products in ranges that are vegan. What you class as a vegan product here is entirely up to you! Within veganism you'll find there are lots of things that you have to decide for yourself, and things that you may find more challenging to decide on then others. To help you out I've made this list below of completely vegan and cruelty free brands. There are a lot of brands out there that are cruelty free with the majority of their products being vegan, but in the interest of clarity for you, I have made a list of purely vegan brands! You can browse these brands with no worries about the bunnies or the rats and you can freely spend your money with no guilt!

Some cruelty free Make up Brands

B. Beauty

Beauty Without Cruelty

Cover FX

Eco Tools

Elf

Hourglass

Inika

Kat Von D

Lily Lolo

Milk Make up

Pacifica

Some not completely vegan companies but cruelty free and vegan options:

Anastasia Beverly Hills

Barry m

Colourpop

Tarte

Gosh

Makeup geek

Nyx

MUA

Pur cosmetics

Revolution

Wetnwild

Please note how these are only some of the brands that are cruelty free or vegan! I put the ones that I think are most popular and accessible for people to investigate! There are lots of brands out there and I don't want this list to be dragged out over the span of five or six pages! Here are some good websites with a lot more companies –

https://www.crueltyfreekitty.com/ultimate-guide-to-cruelty-free-makeup/

https://features.peta.org/cruelty-free-company-search/index.aspx

https://www.buzzfeed.com/izzyhicks/shopping-in-superdrug-your-cruelty-free-beauty-gu-1vebf?utm_term=.ti28V3PLwM#.mv48ExvJbQ

https://logicalharmony.net/

Part Three - False Eyelashes

There are companies that offer faux mink versions of their mink eyelashes but seeing as they sell products that do support Mink eyelashes add/or animal cruelty I decided to leave them off of this list! Whether you chose to by them or not is your choice.

E.L.F lashes

Huda Beauty Faux Mink Lashes

KoKo Lashes

Nyx Lashes

Superdrug own brand lashes

Unicorn Cosmetics

Violet Voss

Part Four - Bath & Shower Products

Within this 'lifestyle' section of veganism you'll come to realise there are lots of chemicals that just are not safe! A lot of brands still test on animals and there are a lot of chemicals that they source from quite frankly weird places. A lot of companies do offer vegan products that are not ragingly expensive and work just as effectively as non-vegan products. Below is a list of some of the shampoos, conditioners and shower gels that are vegan;

Most of Aldi's shower gels – will be labelled on packaging.

Some of Co-ops bath gel, shower gel and own brand soaps.

Faith in Nature products – will be labelled on packaging.

Most Original Source products – Will be labelled on packaging.

Some Lush products – can be checked in store or online.

Some Superdrug products – will be labelled on packaging.

Most Treaclemoon products – will be labelled on packaging.

Pacifica – completely vegan brand.

Some Nature's Gate products – information on their website.

Beauty without Cruelty – completely vegan.

Some Dr Organics products – information online.

Bulldog- beard shampoo & conditioner & shower gel.

Most of the Soap Co products – information on their website.

Dr Bronner's – mostly vegan, information on their website.

Some Puracy products – information on their website.

Some JASÖN products – will be labelled on packaging.

Some of the Maldon Soap Company products – information on their website.

Part Five - Deodorants

Lots of deodorant brands are not cruelty free and vegan, due to the fact armpits are a sensitive area and instead of just cutting out the middle man (being animals) and are just testing it on humans, bunnies and similar animals are caught in the crossfire. A lot of people believe that if you are eating a healthy vegan diet that you don't even need deodorant... In case you aren't one of those people, here are a list of some vegan deodorants;

Bulldog

Faith in nature

Salt of the Earth

Schmidt's Natural Deodorant

Some Dr Organic roll-ons

Superdrug own brand roll-ons

Part Six - Skin Care

Skin care products like cleansers, scrubs, toners, moisturisers, facemasks etc, can also be a bit of a trouble for vegans! Below is a list of some vegan products that are safe to use! Please remember these lists are just some of your options! You will be able to find more out there.

Botanical Signature

Bulldog

Dr Bronner's

Fair Squared

Most Superdrug own brand products

Some Puracy products

Some JASÖN products

Some Lush products

Some Freeman Beauty products

Some Mount Purious products

Pacifica

Part Seven - Dental Care

A list of products that will help you keep your dental hygiene spot on! This list includes; toothpaste, tooth powders, mouth wash and dental flosses.

Co-op Own Brand

Dr Bronner's

KingFisher

Most AloeDent products

Sarakan

Some Lush products

Superdrug own brand products

Part Eight -Perfumes

Aromi Beauty

Aura Cacia

Dolma Perfumes/Afershaves

Eden Perfumes/Aftershaves

Jack Black

Lush

Scent and Colour

Stella McCartney

Pacifica Beauty Perfume

Part Nine – Vitamin Tablets

Lots of people struggle with how to go about their vitamins and minerals! Some people don't bother taking vitamins and others do, once again it is your personal choice! I have always taken multivitamins and iron, so you bet that didn't change just because I went vegan. So below is going to be a list of vegan friendly multivitamins (or places you can go to get them).

Holland and Barrett

Holland and Barrett are very good for labelling which of their tablets are vegan friendly, and if you are not sure there is always staff around to help! So if you get the chance pop into their and see what they can recommend (H&B is also a hive for vegan skin care, deodorants and toothpastes).

Superdrug

In a similar fashion to Holland and Barrett, Superdrug are brilliant and listing which of their vitamins and tablets are vegan friendly!

They also almost always have some sort of offer going on so they are definitely worth the try!

Some brands for you

Country Life – labelled vegan specific.

MyVitamins - labelled vegan specific.

Cytoplan - labelled vegan specific.

Deva - labelled vegan specific.

MRM – labelled vegan specific.

B12

You can get tablets for B12 from a lot of good vegan brands and it is very important that you ensure that you keep *all* your essential vitamins up to a good standard. B12 is something that some people find they don't get a lot or enough of as a vegan, so you should make sure you are getting enough.

Symptoms of lack of B12 could be any of the following; Weakness, tiredness, or light-headedness

Heart palpitations and shortness of breath, constipation, diarrhoea, loss of appetite, or gas, nerve problems like numbness or tingling, muscle weakness, and problems walking.

Obviously if you experience any of these don't just go pop some B12 check with your doctors in case it could be anything else!

Part Ten- Extra Vegan Bathroom Treats

Now this section here is dedicated to your extra bits and pieces you'll more than likely find in your bathroom! There are vegan versions of almost everything as you are about to see, take your time to switch your old products up for new products in all these areas! A lot of these brands do carry more than what I am listing, I want to just make it apparent to you what the little 'extra' things they carry are!

Fair Squared – Condoms, period cups & intimate care.

Glyde – Condoms.

Veeda – Tampons.

Diva Cup – Menstrual cup.

Mooncup – Menstrual cup.

Dr Bronner's – Hand sanitiser & shaving gel.

Green People – Sun care & shaving creams.

Attitude – Sun care.

Green People – Sun care.

JASÖN – Sun Care.

Some Puracy Products – Baby care/ bug repellent.

Ecozone – Baby care products.

All Good – Herbal pain relief spray.

PETA Vegan Lip Balm – Lip balms (Obviously).

Hurraw! Balm – Lip balm.

Some Lush products – Lip scrubs, lip balms and hand soaps.

Cotton & Bamboo – Planet friendly cotton buds.

Humble Brush – Bamboo toothbrush.

Part Eleven - The Vegan Life Hack

(Well standard life hack, let's be honest)

Coconut oil is a blessing when it comes to beauty and hygiene. Some of its uses are;

A moisturiser

Make up remover

Teeth Whitener

Lip Balm

Hand/nail oil

Soothe stretch marks

Massage oil

Conditioning treatment for your hair

To clean your hands of dirt, glue or paint

Dandruff relief

Acne relief

Eczema relief

Sunburn relief

Shaving cream

Cracked heel

(In a slight side note it can also be very helpful for dogs as it is good for their coat and contains lauric acid which is good for building a strong immune system.)

As you can see, there is a lot to think about when you are evaluating the health and beauty side of products! There are loads of options out there for you to explore and get your hands on so don't be afraid to try new or different products.

Don't let yourself get overwhelmed at all these products you have never even looked at or thought twice about before, veganism is a whole new lifestyle and a complete 180 (probably) on what you know, it is not something that you have to achieve overnight.

House & Home

A lot of things fill your home, and surprisingly, a lot of them are not vegan friendly. Well, not really. This section will help you replace your cleaning products, your washing powders, your candles and anything else that may not necessarily be vegan. This is where you start to realise you have reached the goal, you are becoming an as well-rounded vegan as you possibly can! You eat cruelty free, you look, smell and feel cruelty free (that doesn't sound as appealing as I hoped it would) and now you're looking to make your home cruelty free. This section may get to be a touch 'bits-and-bobs', but it will be worth it I promise! Just have a look at the titles and see which things appeal to you and which don't, and you'll have filled your home in vegan products in no time!

Once you've made it through this section we're going to be addressing a lot of questions, debates and issues veganism raises for the individual. This is just a guide, and I am not sitting with you, you are more than free to skip to that section now, it really is your personal decision. But if you do decide to stay, here is some cruelty free products for the home.

A lot of the companies and brands on these lists are considered 'big' brands, please remember that you can find small products or small companies scattered around your local area that will offer you good quality vegan cruelty free products!

*Disclaimer – there can be issues with parent companies and their ethics when it comes to products like cleaning products, I have tried my best to include *only* entirely safe products*

Part One - Cleaning Products

This section will include companies that have vegan products such as; multipurpose sprays, kitchen cleaners, toilet cleaners, bleaches, polishes, stain removers and floor cleaners:

Bio D

Citra Solv

Dr Bronner's

Ecoegg

ECOS

Ecozone

Greenscents

Method

Sun and Earth

 (Some) Puracy products

Part Two - Laundry Products

This section will include products such as; laundry liquid, laundry balls, laundry tablets/capsules, stain remover, fabric conditioner, towel softeners and dryer cubes.

Bio D washing powder

Ecoleaf washing powder

Ecozone

Greenscents

Home Solv

(Some) Puracy products

Part Three - Cleaning Tools

A lot of brands are vegan by default. Here is a list of some that are 100% certified vegan.

Eco Egg – Reusable kitchen towels.

Ecoforce – **Recycled** cloths, scourers & washing up brushes.

Ecozone – Sponges and cloths.

LoofCo – Scrubbing brushes.

Part Four - Other Vegan Household Products

Air Scense (owned by Citra Solv) – Air freshener.

Ecos – Drain cleaners, fruit and vegetable wash and pet products.

Ecoforce – **Recycled** pegs.

Ecozone – Descaler products, toilet blocks and spider repellent.

Part Five - DIY Vegan Cleaning Products

A lot of people opt for making their own vegan cleaning products as a way of avoiding any toxic chemicals and as a way of ensuring they know exactly what goes into keeping their homes clean. Now, people dabble in this by making their own products from recipes they find online or play around with themselves until they find something effective. Below will be a list of ingredients that you may want to put into your own home-made cleaning products!

Baking soda – Good for cleaning & scouring.

Corn-starch - Can be used for cleaning windows, polish furniture and shampooing carpets.

Lemon Juice – Fantastic at killing/reducing household bacteria.

White Vinegar – Good for use on grease, mildew and odours.

Olive oil – Can be used as a household polish.

Part Six - Vegan Candles

There are some brands of different candles that are not vegan friendly. Surprisingly things like birthday candles, often contain things such as animal fat (yeah, weird, I know) but don't you worry there are still candles that you can find that are safe for you to use! Below is a list of some vegan companies that are safe to use:

ASDA's own brand candles

Happy Bee soy candles

Home Bargains own brand candles

Pacifica

Pure Botanica

Tesco's own brand candles

Yankee Candles (minus the bee wax ones, stay clear of those)

Human/Other Ethics

Part One - Ethical Clothing Companies

A lot of vegans opt to support ethical clothing companies as a part of their lifestyle. Ethical fashion has been described as 'an approach to the design, sourcing and manufacture of clothing which maximises benefits to people and communities while minimising impact on the environment.'[26] and is a means of ending 'fast fashion'. According to the *Ethical Fashion Forum* there are three types of fast fashion; social, environmental and commercial, all three of these can tackle issues such as; fast fashion, unfair wages, toxic pesticides and chemicals, water use, recycling and sustainability. Ethical fashion is important to consider as it is something that is easily overlooked. What we wear can has a massive impact on the planet, the people and what we promote as normal and acceptable. The idea of fast fashion and ethical fashion is something that everyone (not only vegans) should consider as if we raise the barrier for standards of companies and their ethics. Below is a list of some ethical clothing companies/companies working towards ethical guidelines or standards for you to have a look at:

I have included some high street brands collections in here just to show that you can accessibly find ways to be more conscious of the clothes you are wearing

---

[26] Ethical Fashion Forum, http://www.ethicalfashionforum.com/the-issues/ethical-fashion (Accessed 15/06/18)

ASOS recycled denim

Fat Face

Finisterre

H&M's Conscious Exclusive collection

Matt & Nat

Monsoon

New Balance

People Tree

Stella McCartney

Thought Clothing

ThredUP

Toms

As well as investigating brands yourself there is always the option to use charity shops, clothing swaps or simply exchanging clothes with friends.

Part Two - Fairtrade

Fairtrade is very similar to ethical fashion in the sense that it wants to create a sustainable working environment and wants to enable products to be made in a sustainable way. On the Fairtrade Foundations official website[27] you will be able to find lots of information on why Fairtrade is important and how it is affecting people. There is reportedly 'over 4,500 Fairtrade products'[28] on

---

[27] https://www.fairtrade.org.uk/What-is-Fairtrade/Fairtrade-and-sustainability (Accessed 15/06/18)

the market and you can easily identify them by the Fairtrade Logo (see below).

Part Three - Palm Oil

Palm oil is an oil that is very commonly used whether that be in our food, our cosmetics, and our cleaning products or even in our fuels. It has caused a great deal of destruction to the rainforest and it is continuing to do so every day. Palm oil is not only very damaging to the environment when it is used as biofuel; which is damaging to the animals, small holders and indigenous tribes. The palm oil industry is causing 'endangered species such as the orangutans, Borneo elephants and Sumatran tigers are being pushed closer to extinction.'[29] Palm oil has been responsible for reportedly 'more than 700 land conflicts'[30] within Indonesia.

This destruction cannot arguably be something that the vegan movement can support, it is destructive to the planet, the animals and the people who have to live where these palm oil plantations

---

[28] Ibid, (accessed 15/06/18)

[29] https://www.rainforest-rescue.org/topics/palm-oil#start (Accessed 15/06/18)

[30] Ibid

are being created. It is very difficult to go completely palm oil free due to the quantity of it being used in everyday products, however you can do things to reduce your palm oil intake.

http://www.saynotopalmoil.com/What_can_i_do.php .This is a lovely page to go to where you can find out some more information about what you can do to prevent palm oil finding its space in your life. Not only do they have a twenty-eight-day challenge, they have lots of information on palm oil.

Part Five - Plastic Usage Reduction

Non-recyclable plastic is having a massive impact on the oceans and the marine life in the oceans. This is something that everyone can individually work on cutting down (or entirely out) of their lives. 'What's this got to do with veganism?' I hear you ask from the distance; well my friend, it is something that is greatly affecting the planet and its inhabitants, so it is something vegans should form an opinion on. Below is a list with some shocking facts about plastic;

- Roughly 12 million tonnes of plastic end up in the sea per year.[31]
- Roughly 700 different marine species have been found tangled up in plastic[32]
- 91% of plastic waste isn't recycled.[33]

---

[31] Sherrington, Chris, *Plastics in the Marine Environment,* June 2016, http://www.eunomia.co.uk/reports-tools/plastics-in-the-marine-environment/ (Accessed 15/06/18)
[32] http://www.open.ac.uk/research/news/blue-planet (Accessed 15/06/18)

- 'The ocean is expected to contain 1 tonne of plastic for every 3 tonnes of fish by 2025, and by 2050, more plastics than fish (by weight).' [34]
- 'Revealed more than nine billion fewer plastic bags were used since the government introduced a 5p charge, an 83 per cent reduction.' [35]

As you can see, plastic is a major problem for the environment and there are things we can all do to stop contributing to this plastic waste that *will* fill our oceans if we do not step up and do something today.

I have come up with a little list of things you can do to help cut down your plastic usage, a lot of these are day to day things but some are for those of you who are a bit more dedicated:

Ways to reduce your single use plastic use

Buy a reusable water bottle/mug/travel-cup (if you take these into stores you sometimes save yourself some money as well).

Buy Tupperware over single use containers (you can get freezer & microwave safe Tupperware!).

Say **no** to straws.

Buy metal reusable straws (if you can't live without a straw).

Buy on the go cutlery.

Use reusable bags.

---

[33] https://news.nationalgeographic.com/2017/07/plastic-produced-recycling-waste-ocean-trash-debris-environment (Accessed 15/06/18)
[34] World Economy Forum, *The New Plastics Economy Rethinking the future of plastics,* January 2016, P7.
[35] Press Release, *Environment Secretary pledges action on ocean plastics,* 21 July 2017. https://www.gov.uk/government/news/environment-secretary-pledges-action-on-ocean-plastics (Accessed 15/06/18)

Hankies may be old fashion, but they stop you buying single use tissues with plastic packaging when you have a cold!

Buy bamboo toothbrushes.

Buy biodegradable cotton buds.

Buy soap and shampoo bars (reducing the plastic packaging you use).

Buy in bulk grains to avoid excessive packaging.

Buy fruit and veggies out of the plastic.

Questions about Veganism Answered

In this section I will discuss and try to answer some of the most debating questions within the vegan community. There are quite a few of these so you might be here some time, just a heads up. I also would like to just pop in a cheeky disclaimer here? that a lot of the answers to these questions are personal or can be biased, so I will try and address all sides of the argument then end it on what I conclude to be the best answer. As I've said many times within this book, veganism is a personal journey, and many of these questions you will find your own answers too based on your own beliefs and your own journey. Some of these questions are well known for starting debates within the vegan community, so feel free to *debate* about them not argue.

Part One - Some Vegan Life Advice

In this section I am going to offer you some advice in regards to how people around you behave, how you feel about certain aspects in your life and things that may be affecting your transition into veganism! In this section I'm not going to bombard you with facts and studies, I am simply going to offer my limited words of wisdom to you.

I'm going to keep it real with you here, there may be issues your facing that aren't in this section, or I may give you advice that doesn't do shit all to help you. If this is the case, ask another vegan! There are some questions on here that I am in no way qualified to answer as I have not personally been through them! I will try my very best to help answer any of the worries or questions you do have, so please do give this section a little read!

Veganism and Medication

This is an issue that is debated within the vegan community, mainly by your average joes like me and you and militant vegans. A lot (if not all) of prescribed medication is tested on animals and can even contain animal products, which would make them non-vegan friendly. Some people believe this makes you a non-vegan for taking your prescription medication. Now, I know I said I would stay unbiased, but I quite frankly can't with this discussion. If you need your medication, it does not make you non-vegan for taking it. When you have an illness that is not gaining any relief from veganism it is 100% acceptable for you to take your tablets (in fact it is even if you are gaining relief, if you feel you need your tablets just take them ok?). As long as you are doing all you can within your vegan lifestyle to keep animal cruelty at a minimum within your life you are still a vegan in my eyes. Medication does not make you nonvegan. Being ill does not make you nonvegan. Please, do not damage your health because a militant vegan has told you that you cannot care about the animals because you are taking your medication.

Veganism and Vaccinations

Similarly, to the past section, vaccinations are technically not vegan. I saw a tweet the other day which discussed how veganism is about compassion to all beings, and that extends to human beings, so by not getting your child vaccinated you could arguably cause more damage than by getting them vaccinated. It is important to understand in the situation of vaccinations that some people are not vaccinated due to doctor's recommendations or advice. It is important to account for people's personal situations when it comes to things like medications and vaccinations but in my opinion getting your child or self vaccinated does not make you any less vegan.

How to accept that medication doesn't make you any less vegan

With this I would say that you must accept that you must be alive and healthy to even enable yourself to be a vegan. If you are well then you are more able to help educate people and pass on the vegan message, without your medication you may not be in any position to do so.

It is also important to remind yourself that you are already doing everything you can to prevent animals suffering. If you are no longer eating animal products, no longer wearing them, using them, or using products that have caused animals to suffer, you are doing everything within your abilities to enable change. Do not beat yourself up over the one thing that you cannot change.

It can be horrible to have that one thing that you wish you could change, but just remember how much you are doing over the one thing that you cannot.

How to cope in a non-vegan house

My house at home and my house at university are both non-vegan houses. I have always lived with people who have not shared the same morals as me, want to argue with me everyday and/or just don't really give a shit about it. It can be quite difficult to cope with people who are poking everyday at you or even being rude about the fact that they eat animals. I'd say there are three or four separate ways to deal with this, and it is entirely up to you which way you approach it.

The first way to cope with it is to actually discuss things with them. If you can have an adult conversation to them about why you are vegan it make help them to understand your beliefs and morals which *should* result in them at least having a level of respect to you for them.

The second way to try and face their questioning or rudeness towards it is to politely explain to them that it makes you upset when they pick at you and you would appreciate it if they just let you live your life their way and in return you will accept their views. This can be difficult for some people as they have to then accept that someone eats the foods you chose not to, if you can manage to not get upset by it then this can be really affective and making it easy for you to live with meat eaters.

The third way to approach this is to almost make it like banter (jokey and light-hearted for you non-brits), I often opt for this with my flatmates as it makes it a casual way for us to understand each other's dietary choices. Some people don't like this as they feel like it dismisses the cruelty of what they are doing, but a lot of the time it can be used as a friendly and playful gateway into a serious conversation about meat and dairy without anybody feeling like they have been attacked for how they chose to eat.

Finally, you can approach living this way by casually trying to help them understand how they are living is cruel and not good for them! People don't like facts shoved in their face, because they don't like to face them (all tea, all shade). The way I would go about this is by when you make food, offer to cook for them or ask if you can cook something together (by default it must be vegan ha-ha), try and start casual conversations about why they're not vegan and explain to them what you think veganism can do for them etc. It can be difficult to live with people who make jabs at how you chose to live, but there are ways to face them and discuss them without making yourself uncomfortable.

I live with people who won't ever listen to why I am vegan, they just make jabs at me for it, what should I do?

It sounds so very cliché but you have to just ignore them. Some people will never listen, they have to just figure things out on their own. While you are living in their house make sure you just stick to your guns and let them go about their life and you go about yours. If you don't give them a reaction they'll eventually get bored and give up. If they disrespect your food choices, then you need to find your voice and stand up for yourself. Don't let them walk over you if they cannot respect you.

My parents don't want me to go vegan, what do I do?

If you live at home and your parents still cook for you and make your decisions about food, the best thing to do is take control where you can when it comes to animal products. When you are out, at school or buying your own food buy vegan! You can just ask you parents to respect your opinion and just not feed you meat or dairy, I would personally do this one step at a time. Say you currently eat meat, dairy and eggs, I would ask my parents to not give you any meat as you don't want to eat it and you do not want it to go to waste and then gradually work the others out. When I first went vegetarian my parents said they can deal with me being vegetarian, but they could never deal with me being vegan, and then I went ahead and did it. When I explained to them how much better my health is (and when they started to actually see this) they came around to the idea rather quickly. My whole family do still eat meat, but now my mum and dad swap out sausages, mince, meatballs and chicken nuggets for Quorn three to four times a week. If you stay persistent you will be surprised at your parent's response to your diet choices!

How to be: Young and Vegan

I think I have touched on this a bit in my previous answer! Veganism young can be hard as a lot of people think you are too young to make these kinds of decisions. You must stay persistent and keep your head in the right place! Transition at a pace that is comfortable to you and let it be know to the adults and other people in your life that you are going on this journey and you would like them to accept and understand why. Make sure you have your knowledge and facts by your side at all times so you can explain to the people in your life that you are aware what the lifestyle is and what it can do for you. If you are in a situation where your parents, caregiver or elders won't allow you to go vegan, just keep your head up. Remember it is a temporary situation, keep reminding them that you do not want to eat the foods they are trying to give you!

What to do if your friendship group are excluding you because of your lifestyle

Honestly, in this situation, I would say get better friends. You are choosing to live a lifestyle where you cause no suffering, you are not trying to do something evil, dumb or uneducated. If your friends cannot respect the way that you live your life than they are not good people and they are not who you need in your life. Friends are supposed to be supportive and understanding of your choices and the key to any good relationship is respect. If you are not getting respected by the people you consider your friends I would definitely remove them from your life. I would point out here however if you are rude to them about their lifestyle choices it may explain why they are excluding you (I am not saying it is right to exclude you, but nobody wants a friend who is rude to them). If you cannot look past how they live, again, you need new friends. You should never be exploded for your personal choices and you should never have to face your own friends disrespecting you.

You can meet fellow vegans through things like Twitter, Facebook and Instagram and you may even find people in your local area that you can meet! (be safe and careful with this obviously if you are underage tell a parent and only meet people who you *know* are not catfishes, okay? Stay safe.)

The saying that there are plenty of fish in the sea does not have to only reply to your romantic relationships you can and will find friends who are accepting of who you are and how you want to live!

My friends and family are supportive, but they still exclude me as they don't have wider knowledge

Give them the wider knowledge! Plain and simple! You cannot expect people to know everything you know, that is not the way the world works unfortunately.

Goals to help you transition

A lot of people like to this as a way of helping themselves stay motivated! There are several well-known ways to approach this such as; Veganuary, Meatless Mondays, Meatless March and Februdairy (which was actually set up by dairy farmers to try and abolish veganism and revive the dying dairy industry, but you bet we took that). There are so many ways you can set goals! I would go for things such as 3 vegan meals a week, going up to 5, 8, 12 and so on! Or I would even start with just doing that as vegetarian and then when you are fully veggie start slowly working out dairy or eggs! Start by trying to only cut out eggs and dairy in ways that are obvious- such as; in cereal, fried eggs or scrambled eggs and then start avoiding things like cakes with those ingredients in! Try replacing your milk and then find yourself meat replacements and then dairy replacements. To conclude, there are lots of ways to set goals within going vegan. I personally would start with whatever feels easiest and the most comfortable for you. Changing your lifestyle can be hard and it is very rare that someone goes perfectly vegan of the bat. Allow yourself some wiggle room and make changes slowly and surely.

How to become an activist

Activism is something that you can do in many ways, shapes and forms! There is anything from becoming a participant in cubes of truth, being a fox hunt sab, stickering, going to vigils, creating art, making vegan YouTube videos, being a vegan chef, having an Instagram about veganism, talking to people about veganism, writing about veganism, tweeting about veganism or even encouraging discussions about veganism to people who may never have spoken about it. You must simply find the way that you find the best for you! Something that you feel comfortable and happy doing. The message of veganism is spread in so many ways, it is almost impossible to not be an activist within the vegan community as not eating, using and condoning animal use is boycotting the industry, you don't have to a James Aspey if you don't want to!

When it comes to actually joining a team of sabs, or a team who do cubes of truth a lot of the time these are accessible to join through Facebook or other forms of social media! A lot of the people who do these types of events are very warm and welcoming and will encourage on their platforms that you join in! Send them a message and ask if you can tag along and I'm sure they will give you the details.

How to not give in to peer pressure

Peer pressure can be difficult as it is a very broad issue. Some people try and pressure you to not go vegan as they think it isn't good for you, others are disrespectful, and others just think it is funny to joke around and they don't realise that you are actually uncomfortable. I personally would say that you need to figure out which of these things your peers are trying to achieve. With the first form of peer pressure, gently remind them that you have done your research, that you are looking out for your health and that you will not let your health deteriorate.

With the people who are just being disrespectful to you, it is important to remind them that it is your choice and it has literally got a whopping 0% chance of affecting their life if they just leave you to it. It can be really difficult when every time you go to your family or see your friends they decide that they are just going to point out your veganism and try and persuade you to go back to something you have morally decided to avoid! Just stick to your guns, remind them it isn't their choice and leave them to it!

With the people who are making you uncomfortable it is important you determine whether or not they respect you. If they respect you, you can take them to the side and ask them to stop as it is not making you feel comfortable and happy. If they are not someone who respects, you the best thing to do is just violently ignore them and everything they have to say. Eventually they will get bored of not getting any sort of response out of you and they will leave you alone.

I find that the best thing to do in these situations is really assess whether these people are the time of people you should be spending your time with and/or on. There is no need for anyone to ever be made uncomfortable when all they are trying to do is reduce suffering and change their own life.

How do I control myself when I'm drunk?

So, we've all done something when we're drunk that we regret in the morning, it becomes an issue when it becomes a repeat offence (and yes this does apply to more than just veganism). The first thing you need to do is remind yourself it is just a slip up and there is no need to beat yourself up about it. The second thing I would do is remind myself why I am going vegan or why I am vegan. watch some documentaries again, read some books, watch some YouTube videos, watch some slaughterhouse footage (if it will reinforce your views) and get yourself back on track. The best way for someone to have 'control' is for the person to have firm beliefs. If your morals and beliefs are firmly in place and in check you will have no issues trying to control yourself.

How do I deal with meat cravings?

A lot of people have meat cravings early on in their vegan journey, it is completely normal. This is because the chances are you were raised eating meat, your body is not used to not having it, so it creates these cravings to remind yourself it is something that you eat. The first way I recommend you cope with this is by, of course, transitioning! Slowly work the products out of your diet and you will find that your body is tricked into thinking it was never even there! This can be one of the most effective ways to avoid cravings as your body gets use to the other products taking the place of meat! Another fantastic way to cope with these cravings is by have your morals in the back of your mind at all time! If you remember why you are not eating meat it makes it that much easier to resist! Secondly, try to get fake meats that are desired to replicate meat as a way of tricking your body into thinking that it is still getting these meats! You can also try eating 'meat' tasting things! For example, a lot of chicken super noodles are vegan, bacon rasher crisps can be vegan, Walkers/Lays roast chicken crisps (and a couple of other meat flavours) are in fact safe for us vegans! Make sure you feed the cravings with foods that are safe for you! Once you are over the initial cravings I promise you it is like the door to veganism opens!

Part Two - Questions You Might Ponder as a Vegan

In this section, I will address questions that most vegans wonder about themselves. This may consist of questions you see as obvious, things you've never thought about and questions that may just leave you debating everything you've ever known. A lot of these questions can encourage great debates, to say the least, so I am going to try to present a non-bias argument for you, so you can make your own decisions (so nobody come for me in the DMs ok?). I'm going to post the issue and then add my opinion on the bottom and my justification as to why, I debated how to present this section for a while and I concluded that this will be the best way for me personally to face the issue! For things that I don't have an opinion of or things that I am unsure of myself I will make sure to state and explain why I feel that way about the issue. A lot of these are very much issues that you would have to decide upon in your own mind, so please take my opinion with a pinch of your own salt.

Is it vegan to have non-vegan pets?

Issue explained - There is a lot of debate around this issue as if you have, for example, a cat or a dog its diet normally consists of meat. Issues stem from this as firstly if you have raised an animal eating meat then it can have a damaging affect to change their diet especially if they have grown very accustom to the diet you feed them. However, some people argue that an animal can thrive on a vegan diet, so there is no excuse to not be feeding your pets a vegan diet.

My opinion - If you don't want to feed an animal meat, do not get a pet that is required to eat meat. If you have had your pet a long time, see no issues with it or you need a pet that is required to eat meat (guide dogs etc) then you can continue to do so. The issue with pets and meat is a personal decision to make, the way I see it being resolved is by people making their own moral decision about their pets and their diets.

Is second hand leather vegan?

The issue - This is debated a lot as it could be argued that second hand leather is vegan because you are not the one directly paying the company to put the item into production, the animal already died for the product and the fact that the suffering technically was not directly supported by you. It can also be argued that second hand leather is vegan as otherwise the product will go to waste and seeing as the animal already died it should be used correctly. On the other side, it is argued that we have no purpose for second hand leather as vegans, if you come into some you can always rehome the item, you can also wear faux leather if you like the look and through wearing leather you are supporting the industry.

My opinion – I personally wouldn't want to wear second hand leather as I feel like it is supporting the industry as it keeps the leather in circulation. I would opt for faux leather if I was after the leather look! However, I do agree that your previous purchases that are non-vegan are something that *you* personally must decide what you want to do with. Some continue wearing them as to not waste them or simply because they cannot afford to replace them, others sell them, and some give them to charities. I think either way the product shouldn't be wasted.

Is honey vegan?

The issue – another topic that often divides the vegan community! It is argued regularly as it can be explained that bees are not harmed in the production of honey so therefore it is safe to eat as a vegan. Others say it is fine to only eat local honey as that supports local beehive keepers (which is something we need to be doing due to the recent decline of bees!). There are discussions against honey as it has been reported that sometimes beekeepers destroy the wings of the queen bee so she cannot leave the hive and therefore keeps the hive in production, and that honey is still an animal by-product that we do not need.

My opinion – I personally wouldn't eat honey as it is an animal by-product. Bees need honey for themselves and we do not need it.

Is it vegan to eat the eggs of your own chickens?

The issue – eggs are something that hens naturally lay so is it safe for vegans to eat them if they come from their own pet chickens? Hens only lay eggs until they have a 'full nest' which is something the egg industry interrupts as they constantly remove their eggs. When you have your own pet chickens you would be affectively doing the same thing, but your chickens are happy healthy and (if you are a good pet parent) free to do as they please, within reason. So, it is therefore safe for an individual to eat their own pet chickens' eggs. Some however argue that this is not true as you still keep your hen in a cycle similar to the egg industry in the sense that they are continuously worked, and they have no rest from laying their eggs. On the health side, it is also illegal to call eggs healthy, therefore why would you even want to eat their eggs?

My opinion – I would not eat the eggs purely because I think eggs are nasty (which they 100% are I will fight over this). On the cruelty side of things, it is a bit more difficult as it is not fair to keep the hen working and keep taking away her eggs, but they are in conditions of love, security and happiness. I personally think that if you are one of those people who cannot give up eggs it is better to use your own hen's eggs, but I think it would be better for you to let the hen live her natural life without your interruption.

Is it vegan to eat products that 'may contain milk'?

The issue – when a product says it 'may contain milk' but is entirely vegan the rest of the way it means it is made in a factory that handles products that contain milk. They put the label there to protect themselves from situations where say a lactose intolerant person has a reaction to their supposed milk free product. Some say this risk of contamination is not vegan and arguably it is supporting a nonvegan company. Others say that this label is just a warning from the company merely to protect themselves, the chances of cross-contamination are so small it is not worth worrying about.

My opinion – I think they are safe to eat, as there are *loads* of vegan products with that label on, you just must be aware of the risks you are taking when that label is present! I think that you have to remember as well that a lot of cheap and cheerful foods have this on their packaging and eating food at that sort if cost can be the only way that some people can afford to be vegan.

Is it vegan to get animals put down who are suffering?

The issue – if an animal is old, ill and unhappy it is a decision you have to make as an owner as to whether or not you let that animal go or you keep it alive. This is an issue as if you put the animal down you are technically killing an animal but if you keep it alive you are also allowing an animal to suffer. This also causes debate as people discuss the actual chances of you 'not being able to help' as a lot of the time people dismiss things such as money, time and other commitments. It has also been argued that it does not matter how much money, time or care you can give to an animal if they are suffering it is selfish to try and prolong their suffering and it becomes the most loving thing to do for the animal (and often others) to put the animal to sleep. The issue of animal euthanasia comes as a debate that can cause vegans a lot of stress as you have to try and figure out what is the most loving thing to do whilst they keep their actions in line with their morals.

My opinion – if there is no way to give an animal live a carefree and happy life, I do believe it is the right thing to do to put an animal down. I think if you have a pet that you know is suffering it is the most loving thing to do. I personally think this because I've had a lot of discussions about human euthanasia and how if someone knows they are terminal what would be the most loving thing for us to do. It can be very difficult to decide what to do with the little beings who you love, but you must do what you see as best by them and nobody deserves disrespect for that. So please, if you do disagree with my view, if someone has had their pet put to sleep, show some compassion and do not attack them for their choices.

Should all vegans be activists?

The issue – this debate normally stems from those who initially went vegan for the animals. The idea of it is that everyone should be going out and trying to spread the vegan message as they have the voice to do that (many vegans refer to themselves as 'the voice for the voiceless'). Seeing as we are the ones who want to prevent cruelty we should be pushing ourselves to communicate this message to others and we should be working hard to keep more and more animals safe from the cruel reality of animal agriculture.

My opinion – I believe that not everyone can be an activist in the sense that they can't go out and do cube of truth or speak to the public. I do however believe that every vegan can be an activist within their own rights. As I discussed earlier on in the book, there are so many ways to be a vegan activist and everyone can find their own way to help! It is not something that is exclusive, people feel like they can share a message in so many different ways and I think it's fantastic that there are so many different forms of activism!

Is it vegan to buy animal products for others?

The issue – some argue that it is not vegan to buy animal products for others at it means that you have contributed to the suffering of animals. However, this is an issue that brings up many questions such as who is it for? Why are you buying them? And even are they going to give you the money for it? It is an issue that caused a big drama on the social media side of veganism and caused a lot of debates in morals and ethics. Some argue that there are situations where this is an okay thing to do as it something you cannot avoid others entirely refuse to go near the idea of buying someone else an item with animal products in.

My opinion – I think this is an issue that takes a lot of understanding of context and why or how you are buying these products. For example, if I asked a homeless person if they wanted a sandwich and I went into the store and there were no vegan options, I would be being cruel to not purchase the person a sandwich, so I would then buy them a non-vegan product. Now if that sort of compassion makes me non-vegan then so be it, but I believe this issue is something that is very subjective and cannot be applied broadly.

Should vegans have non-vegan partners?

The issue – to be honest with you, this one is a bit weird to me, so I will struggle to actually explain the issue I'll have to explain what I believe the issue to be? In a broad sense I think people see it as a problem as you can put your money towards non-vegan products for this person or you risk a higher chance of cross-contamination maybe?

My opinion – I think it's fine to have a non-vegan partner as it is completely your choice to make not mine. If you chose to only date vegans again that is your choice not mine. I think with this issue you have to remember that it isn't your decision who somebody else dates and just because it doesn't fit your preference it doesn't mean you are right.

Should animals be working in industries like the police?

The issue – the vegan approach to this would explain that animals are not ours to work. They should not be forced to work, it is arguably the same as how animals are made to 'work' within the circus. However, some argue that for example, police dogs can be very well loved by their owners and they are treated with the upmost respect. It is also argued that these animals are a necessity for daily life and help industries like the police, bomb disposal and other missions.

My opinion – it is difficult as these animals can be of great help to us, but I don't believe it is fair to make an animal work when they are not designed for work. This can cause some blurred lines however as guide dogs are technically worker dogs, but they are well loved, respected and happy. It all comes down to the treatment of the animal to me personally.

Are Zoos vegan?

The issue – Zoos can be a very cruel place for animals to live as they may be kept in small cages away from their natural habitat and treated very unfairly. Zoos are also a way for us to use animals for our own entertainment, where as in the wild if we see them it is more often by chance and they are wild and free. However, on the other side of the argument some people say that animals *need* to be kept away from the wild due to things such as hunters, poachers and a way of aiding the population. Some 'zoos' are more like rehabilitation centres where the animals are cared for then gradually released back into the wild.

My opinion – Zoos can be a difficult subject, as some zoos are very disgusting towards their animals and others are doing everything they can to keep the animals safe, happy and as 'wild' as they can be. I believe that the issue with zoos is very subjective as we need to be doing things to protect these animals, but there are other means to do so that would be more positive for the animals. It again is something that requires a bit more context as to whether the zoo is a zoo or if it's a shelter, a rehab, a rescue facility or just for pure human entertainment.

Is palm oil vegan?

The issue – Palm oil does not contain any animal by-products, but it is responsible for a lot of destruction and habitat lost. With the extent of the destruction it is debatable whether or not using or buying products that use palm oil is vegan friendly.

My opinion – I believe palm oil in itself is vegan as it has no animal by-products, but I do believe if you can you should be avoiding palm oil as much as you possibly can as it is causing destruction to the wildlife that no animal lover should ever support. Palm oil can be very destructive (more information further into the book) so I believe we should be trying *very* hard to reduce our palm oil usage.

Is it vegan to eat food that contains animal products that would be wasted otherwise?

The issue – If a food is not vegan-friendly and you accidentally purchase it you might find yourself in a situation where you have nobody else to give the food too but you do not want to cause any waste. If you are in this situation you have to pick between eating it or wasting the product.

My opinion- I think you would struggle to find yourself in a situation where you have a non-vegan food and nobody else to give it too. But, if for some strange reason you ended up in this situation I think it is a very personal decision to make. A lot of people have been in this situation in there time as a vegan and everybody reacts differently. It is an issue that is very subjective as it can depend on things like; the persons situation, what product it is, how much it costs and why you can't give it to someone else!

Is it vegan to work somewhere that sells animal products like fish and chip shops or bait stores?

The issue – If you are working somewhere that sells animal products then you arguably helping a company bring in money towards animal cruelty. However, it would be very difficult to find a job that handled absolutely no animal products what so ever (especially in the retail & food industries).

My opinion- It does not make you non-vegan to work somewhere that handles non-vegan products. At the end of the day people everywhere are struggling to find jobs and you should be grateful that you have one. If you have issues with other people working in an industry that can involve animal products, then you can get over it, you have no right to tell someone that the place they may *have* to work makes them any less of a vegan than another place.

Is it vegan to use means of control on animal populations?

The issue – Controlling animal populations can involve cruelty and can be argued to be us intervening and manipulating the wildlife. However, it can also be argued that control of the animal population is something that we need to do to co-exist with the animals that are around us. It can be argued to be non-vegan as it may involve killing animals, causing animals distress or hurting animals.

My opinion – I think we shouldn't use means of animal control that will cause more damage than good, but I understand why some believe that we should be putting in our own efforts so control wildlife. All in all, I have never seen an issue with any of the wild animals that live around me and I think their populations seem to manage themselves, so I personally don't think we need to do anything to control populations. Whether it is vegan or not I believe is all down to the methods that's used to do so.

Part Three - Debunking the most common Anti-Vegan Arguments

Now as a vegan you will find all of a sudden you know a load of nutritionists, environmentalists and advocates for the animal agriculture industry. In this section I will help you to debunk their argument using facts, figures and information! The best way to respond to someone who is trying to argue your point is by having more knowledge than them. Without further ado, this is some of the most popular anti vegan arguments debunked:

Where do you get your protein from?

Protein is something that is one hundred percent accessible for vegans. You can find protein in a lot of plant-based foods and most of them come without the negative side affects that proteins like chicken may have. Below are some images showing the potential foods that you can get your protein from as someone who eats a plant-based diet.

Figure 6 Katie, Plant Based Protein, (April 8, 2014). (Accessed 13/06/18) - http://vecchioneplasticsurgeryblog.com/plant-based-protein/

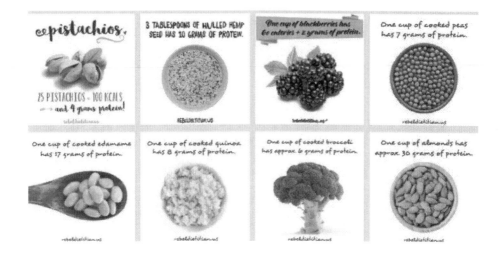

Figure 7 https://www.carlagoldenwellness.com/2015/07/20/plant-sources-of-protein-building-blocks-amino-acids/ (Accessed 13/06/18)

But animals eat other animals?

This is a fact, you cannot argue that this is not a fact. However, you can argue that animals only kill for survival and instinct. It has been known for animals to eat their own offspring if they are hungry, something we see as not morally correct in any way shape or form. Therefore, we cannot dictate our own moral code on an animals moral code is. The simplest way to address this argument is to remind your anti-vegan friend that we do not eat meat for survival. We do not hunt and kill our meat and animals are not our only choice of food. In fact, when you pop down to your local shop to hunt your meat, you find that you aren't about to just eat it raw because your hungry, you'll probably freeze it for another day.

Another good case to bring up here is the story of a child, a rabbit and an apple. If you leave a child in a room with a rabbit and an apple, odds are they will play with the rabbit and eat the apple when they are hungry, not the other way around. Our instincts are simply different to that of a wild animal.

We are the top of the food chain, shouldn't we be eating animals?

It has recently been discovered that we actually are not at the top of the food chain we in fact sit 'somewhere between pigs and anchovies'[36] . Interestingly how we are placed on the same level as pigs isn't it? The discovery of us being is supported by a study conducted by the National Academy of Sciences of the United States, concluded we are not in the top rankings of the food chain and we sit more comfortably in the middle.[37] So that nicely debunks any idea of us being at the top of any food chain. It also becomes a very heated debate if you remind them that we are equal to pigs on the feed chain so by eating them, it is ok to eat our equals?

Circle of life isn't it?

The circle of life refers to *natural* death or a death caused by another animals instincts, something that is not what happens for neatly packaged bits of meat to get into your home.

Eating meat is natural

There are lot of things in the world that are considered 'natural' that we no longer do (see how our appendix no longer has any use within our bodies). We are a species who pride ourselves on moving forward and adapting – for example, we use arguably

[36] Doucleff, Micaheleen, *Between Pigs And Anchovies: Where Humans Rank On The Food Chain,* December 8th 2013, (accessed 13/06/18) https://www.npr.org/sections/thesalt/2013/12/08/249227181/between-pigs-and-anchovies-where-humans-rank-on-the-food-chain

[37] Bonhommeau et al, *Eating up the world's food web and the human trophic level,* University of Arizona: USA, 2013) (Accessed 13/06/18) http://www.pnas.org/content/early/2013/11/27/1305827110

'unnatural' things such as planes, cars, medicines and we operate. Therefore, the argument that we should do what is seen as 'natural' would be disqualified by our own evolution.

But we were designed to eat meat

We'll address this by a simple comparison between meat eaters, herbivores and humans. We'll start of with how meat eaters' physical bodies are designed.

Meat eaters have the following physical features; claws, sharp front teeth, have strong hydrochloric acid in their stomach in order to digest meat, have an intestinal tract that is three times their body length as a way of aiding their digestion, and perspire through their tongue because they have no skin pores.

Herbivores have the following physical features; no claws, no sharp front teeth and rear flat molars for grinding food, have stomach acid that is 20 times weaker than that of meat-eaters, have intestinal tract 10-12 times the length of their body perspire through their skin pores and cool down through sweating,

Humans have the following physical features; no claws, no sharp front teeth and rear flat molars for grinding food, have a stomach acid that is 20 times weaker than that of meat-eaters, have intestinal tract 10-12 times the length of their body, perspire through skin pores and cool down through sweating.[38]

---

[38]Information found on the following sources
http://kitchenoflove.org/sentient-vegetarian-diet/herbivores-or-carnivores/ & https://celestialhealing.net/physicalveg3.htm

Basic Anatomy Chart of carnivores, omnivores, herbivores, frugivores and Humans (two images below)[39]

Dietary Class:	Carnivore	Omnivore	Herbivore	Frugivore	Human
Anatomy:					
Optimal Diet:	Meat	Meat and plants	Leafy plants and grasses	Fruits, veggies, nuts legumes and seeds	Fruits, veggies, nuts, legumes and seeds
Vision (mammals):	Does not see in full color-scale	Does not see in full color-scale	Sees in full color-scale	Sees in full color-scale	Sees in full color-scale
Brain Chemistry:	Fueled by fats and proteins	Fueled by fats and proteins	Fueled by glycogen	Fueled by glycogen	Fueled by glycogen
Circadian Rhythm (mammals):	Sleep 18-20 hours per 24-hour cycle	Sleep 18-20 hours per 24-hour cycle	Sleep 8 hours or less per 24-hour cycle	Sleep 8 hours or less per 24-hour cycle	Sleep 8 hours or less per 24-hour cycle
Mouth Opening Vs. Head Size:	Large	Large	Small	Small to medium	Small
Jaw Type:	Lower jaw embedded inside of upper jaw	Lower jaw embedded inside of upper jaw	Upper jaw sits on the bottom jaw	Upper jaw sits on the bottom jaw	Upper jaw sits on the bottom jaw
Jaw Angle:	Not expanded	Not expanded	Expanded	Expanded	Expanded
Jaw Joint Location:	On the same plane as the molar teeth	On the same plane as the molar teeth	Above the plane of the molar teeth	Above the plane of the molar teeth	Above the plane of the molar teeth
Jaw Motion And Mastication:	Shears meat and swallows; no lateral or forward mobility for chewing	Shearing & crushing; minimal to no lateral or forward mobility for chewing	Great lateral and forward mobility for chewing leafy green plants and grasses	Great lateral and forward mobility for chewing fruit, seeds, nuts and vegetation	Great lateral and forward mobility for chewing fruit, seeds, nuts and vegetables
Neccesity Of Chewing Food:	None; swallows food whole	Swallows food whole &/or simple crushing	Extensive chewing neccesary	Extensive chewing neccesary	Extensive chewing neccesary
Facial Muscles:	Reduced to allow wide mouth gape	Reduced to allow wide mouth gape	Well-developed to facilitate chewing	Well-developed to facilitate chewing	Well-developed to facilitate chewing
Major Jaw Muscles:	Temporalis	Temporalis	Masseter and Pterygoids	Masseter and Pterygoids	Masseter and Pterygoids
Teeth (canines):	Long, sharp, curved fangs	Long, sharp, curved fangs	Rudimentary, dull and short or none	Dull and short or long (for defense)	Rudimentary, short and blunted
Teeth (incisors):	Short and pointed	Short and pointed	Broad, flattened and spade-shaped	Broad, flattened and spade-shaped	Broad, flattened and spade-shaped
Teeth (molars):	Sharp, jagged and blade-shaped	Sharp blades and/or flattened	Flattened with cusps vs. complex surface	Flattened with nodular cusps	Flattened with nodular cusps
Tongue:	Extremely rough for use in tearing meat	Moderate to rough	Moderate to rough	Smooth; used mainly like a shovel for food	Smooth; used mainly like a shovel for food
Salivary Gland Size:	Small	Small	Large	Large	Large
Salivary Chemistry:	Acidic	Acidic	Alkaline	Alkaline	Alkaline
Salivary Enzymes:	No carb-digesting enzymes; lysosomes	No carb-digesting enzymes; lysosomes	Has carb-digesting enzymes like ptyalin	Has carb-digesting enzymes like ptyalin	Has carb-digesting enzymes like ptyalin
Stomach Capacity:	60-70% of total vol. of digestive tract	60-70% of total vol. of digestive tract	Less than 30% of tot. vol. of digestive tract	21-27% of total vol. of digestive tract	21-27% of total vol. of digestive tract
Stomach Acidity:	Less than or = pH 1 with food in stomach	Less than or = pH1 with food in stomach	pH 4 to 5 with food in stomach	pH 4 to 5 with food in stomach	pH 4 to 5 with food in stomach
Peristalsis:	Does not require fiber to stimulate	Does not require fiber to stimulate	Requires fiber to stimulate	Requires fiber to stimulate	Requires fiber to stimulate
Length Of Small Intestine:	1.5 to 3 times body-length	3 times body-length	20 times body-length	9 times body-length	9 times body length

---

[39] https://pupaveg.deviantart.com/art/Basic-anatomy-chart-711602481
(Accessed 13/06/18)

Colon Type:	Simple	Simple	Complex	Complex	Complex
Colon Length:	Short	Short	Long	Long	Long
Colon Shape:	Smooth	Somewhat sacculated	Sacculated	Sacculated	Sacculated
Colon Chemistry:	Alkaline	Alkaline	Acidic	Acidic	Acidic
Liver Type:	Complex with 5 distinct chambers	Complex	Simple	Simple	Simple
Liver Size:	Proportionally 50% larger than others	Proportionally larger than herbivores	Slightly larger than frugivores	Proportionally relatively small	Proportionally relatively small
Bile Flow:	Comparatively heavy	Comparatively moderate	Comparatively weak	Comparatively weak	Comparatively weak
Vitamin A (liver detoxification):	Can metabolize large amounts efficiently	Can metabolize large amounts efficiently	Can only metabolize smaller amounts eff.	Can only metabolize smaller amounts eff.	Can metabolize smaller amounts eff.
Short-Chain Fatty Acids:	Can't convert to LCFAs	Can't convert to LCFAs	Can convert to LCFAs	Can convert to LCFAs	Can convert to LCFAs
Cholesterol:	Can metabolize large amounts efficiently	Can metabolize large amounts efficiently	Can only metabolize phytosterols effic.	Can only metabolize phytosterols effic.	Can only metabolize phytosterols effic.
Uricase:	Renal secretion (kidneys)	Renal secretion (kidneys)	No secretion	No secretion	No secretion
Urinary Concentration:	Extreme	Extreme	Comparatively weak	Moderate	Moderate
Urinary Chemistry:	Acidic	Acidic	Alkaline	Alkaline	Alkaline
Digestion (time to complete):	From 2 to 4 hours	From 6 to 10 hours	From 24 to 48 hours	From 12 to 18 hours	From 12 to 18 hours
Placenta (mammals):	Zonary-shaped	Zonary-shaped	Discoid-shaped	Discoid-shaped	Discoid-shaped
Limbs:	Has 4 paws with claws	Has 4 paws with claws or hooves	Has 4 legs with hooves	Has arms with pre-hensile hands & feet	Has arms with prehensile hands
Locomotion:	Walks on all 4 legs	Walks on all 4 legs	Walks on all 4 legs	Walks on all 4 limbs or upright	Walks Upright
Mammaries:	Multiple teats for nursing litters	Multiple teats for nursing litters	Multiple teats for 1-2 offspring or litters	Dual breasts for nursing 1-2 offspring	Dual breasts for nursing 1-2 offspring
Skin And Hair (mammals):	100% covered in hair	100% covered in hair	Pores with extensive hair covering body	Pores with extensive hair covering body	Pores with minimal hair
Cooling System:	Has sweat glands in paws only; panting	Minimal sweat glands in mammals	Has sweat glands all over the body	Has sweat glands all over the body	Has sweat glands all over the body
Nails:	Sharp claws	Sharp claws or blunt hooves	Blunt hooves	Flattened nails	Flattened nails

As you can see by this anatomy chart we are more atomically similar to herbivores and frugivores over meat eaters.

Farm animals are bred to kill, they will overpopulate the earth if we don't kill them for meat.

Farm animals are genetically 'enhanced' in order for us to produce them for meat, as a side affect of this most of the animals are very ill or disease ridden (think back to the list of illness' in dairy cows I showed you earlier). It is a very cruel practice to bred animals for slaughter purposes or purposes that make them, for example, most can agree dog fighting, bull fighting, and dog racing is wrong and/or harmful for the animals, so we shouldn't allow it simply because it is a different species. The fact that farm animals are bred to kill is a fact, but there are places these animals can go to stay safe (sanctuaries are willing to put in the work to save these animals).

Now the issue with 'overpopulating' and farm animals is one I've thought upon in the past myself. The fact to the matter is that the meat and dairy industry is a demand and supply industry, and the world will not go vegan overnight, therefore their will not be millions of animals roaming the streets. The world was not overpopulated with chickens, cows and sheep before we started to exploit them, if you leave the species to go back to their own, normal, regulated existence, there will be no issue with overpopulation.

Okay, so they won't overpopulate us, but won't they go extinct?

As mentioned above, they would manage their own population, we would no longer be killing them, they would live their natural lives and live in their own herds.

Most of these animals that would be rescued would go into sanctuaries, they wouldn't be released into the wild in some Free Willy type of film, chances are they would be too domesticated and not know how to survive. Within the sanctuary they would breed at their normal rates and the animals and their babies would be cared for.

Meat helped us to evolve from apes and therefore makes us human

This has been debated a lot over the years as it has be recorded that there is evidence that meat made our brains grow to a bigger size. However, there has also been an argument that 'wherever humans have gone in the world, they have carried with them two things, language and fire.'[40] We are the only species that eats

---

[40] Adler, Jerry, *Why Fire Makes Us Human*
Cooking may be more than just a part of your daily routine, it may be what made your brain as powerful as it is, June 2013, (accessed

warm food, so it has been debated whether or not that is the thing that divides us from other animals and what the affect of doing so may be. The idea of cooking influencing our evolution was proposed by Richard Wrangham who was a British primatologist. In Wranghams book *Catching Fire, How Cooking Made us Human* the affect of cooking and food efficiency is discussed.

Veganism Is Expensive

Like any lifestyle, you can make a diet as cheap or as expensive as you *choose* to make it. A vegan diet can be based around staple grains like pasta, rice and potato and beans (some of the cheapest foods there are) and you can shop in season and get your fruit and veg at a cheaper price than normal. Or, you can live off of fake meats, fake cheeses and fancy products! It's entirely up to you how expensive you make the diet. For example, my budget is roughly £2 a day and I live a very happy healthy life on a vegan diet.

Veganism isn't sustainable

This argument is common as all of a sudden people assume the only ones eating avocados and quinoa is vegans, which simply is not true. There has been a vast amount of research conducted into which diet is the most sustainable. One study analysed 14 different diet types and it's affect on things such as water usage and land usage and it concluded that veganism had one of the greatest affects in reducing the usage of these things. The study found that 'The largest environmental benefits across indicators were seen in those diets which most reduced the amount of animal-based foods, such as vegan (first place in terms of benefits for two environmental indicators), vegetarian (first place for one

---

13/06/18)
https://www.smithsonianmag.com/science-nature/why-fire-makes-us-human-72989884/?no-ist,

indicator), and pescatarian (second and third place for two indicators).'[41].

Another study directly compared a meat eating diet to a plant based diet (following the same calorific intake) and found that the meat-based diet required more land, energy and water than the vegan diet.[42]

Where it cannot be disputed that a lot of foods in both diets contain things like chemicals and pesticides it is factual that the vegan diet would safe us a lot of land, water and energy. Both diets need to be working to affectively remove the things that make them unsustainable so that we all follow a diet that will fit with our every growing population.

Bugs die when crops are farmed

No vegan will deny this because it is a fact, but vegans are doing all the can to prevent and reduce as much suffering as humanly possible.

But, if someone really seems to care about the bugs enough to show you statistics and facts about the bugs you are single-handedly killing, remind them that a lot of theses crops are fed to animals, and therefore they are eating not only the animals who died for the fruit vegetables and grains that they eat, but they also have the blood of the meat, and the bugs that died for that on their hands.

Veganism is a placebo though

---

[41] Aleksandrowicz L, Green R, Joy EJM, Smith P, Haines A, *The Impacts of Dietary Change on Greenhouse Gas Emissions, Land Use, Water Use, and Health: A Systematic Review*, 2016.
https://doi.org/10.1371/journal.pone.0165797 (Accessed 15/06/18)
[42] David Pimentel, Marcia Pimentel; Sustainability of meat-based and plant-based diets and the environment, The American Journal of Clinical Nutrition, Volume 78, Issue 3, 1 September 2003, Pages 660S–663S, https://doi.org/10.1093/ajcn/78.3.660S (Accessed 15/06/18)

If you notice any health changes you'll hear this one a lot. People will go on about how it is just a placebo, how now it's helped you can go back or how you must have made other changes. The best way to face this is by reminding them that lots of people report health changes when going vegan (maybe even recommend them some documentaries), and let them know that if you feel healthier that is all that matters. It is your life and your health and as long as you are genuinely healthy and happy it isn't there place to tell you that you are not.

You will hear a lot of arguments in your time as to why you shouldn't be vegan, why bacon is the best thing in the world and why you are an idiot for wanting to reduce suffering, change your health or help the planet. I hope this section has somewhat made you feel equipped to face the angry anti-vegans out there. Remember, always carry your arguments with grace and recognition to what the other is saying, you're not going to get anywhere with any argument by getting angry or personally attacking someone (even if they are doing it to you!).

Part Four - How Veganism makes a Difference

Veganism can be a fantastic aid in helping the planet and all the beings we have the privilege of sharing the earth with. By going vegan, you will be cutting down your water usage, your grain usage and your energy usage. You will be saving animals from suffering and you will be enabling them to have a voice.

It can be very easy to become disheartened and believe that what you are doing will have no effect, but I promise you it does. **You** can be the reason that veganism becomes a discussion to the people around you. **You** can be the reason that one less cow, pig, sheep or chicken has to suffer needlessly. **You** can be the reason that the rainforest is saved sooner. **You** can be the reason that you are at your all time best.

Please always remember why you are going vegan and what you are achieving!

La Fin

You've officially made it! You have finished this guide to veganism. I hope you feel more reassured in your choices, and that you feel more comfortable in your journey into a vegan life.

Remember that you are in no rush to become vegan. You can take this journey at your own pace and you can bring veganism into your life in your own ways, whatever makes you feel comfortable and at ease is what is best for you will you are making these changes. Life changes can be very scary and sometimes it can feel like you aren't ever making progress or any differences but you have to keep reminding yourself why you are doing what you are doing. Veganism is so much more than just a diet, it is a lifestyle. It is a way of thinking, a way of being and a way of existing.

I would like to take a moment to thank you for your purchase of this book and thank you for taking your time to give it a read. I sincerely hope that I have helped you take steps on your journey and I hope that my passion for the movement has helped spark any sort of inspiration in your life.

As previously mentioned I will be leaving means of contact on the next page in case you feel you need anymore help on your journey.

Good luck and remember that you are in control of what you eat, how you live and how you feel.

Amy Kennedy

Twitter - @amyythevegan

Instagram - @amykennedywriting

Email –
amykennedypoetry@hotmail.com

Made in the USA
Middletown, DE
21 September 2018